Rafazh Francisco Carmona

THE IRON STALLION

AN AMERICAN LOVE STORY

By Rafael Francisco Carmona

HIRSHBERG PUBLISHING, INC.

Warning-Disclaimer

This publication is not intended to be an instructional guide and/or a safety manual regarding the operation of motorcycles. This publication contains excerpts and quotes from certain individuals interviewed by the author and such views as expressed in this book by such individuals are personal to such individuals so interviewed. Neither the author or publisher have attempted to verify or test the accuracy or validity of any of the safety or operational views and/or opinions expressed by individuals interviewed for this book, and accordingly the accuracy and completeness, and the opinions based thereupon, are not guaranteed or warranted in any manner by the publisher and/or the author. Accordingly, the publisher and author expressly disclaim any responsibility for the accuracy, completeness and/or validity of any such safety and/or operational views or opinions so expressed herein. This book should not be used as an instruction or operational manual or text. If you do not wish to be bound by the above, you may return this book to the publisher for a full refund.

For information contact:
Ron S. Hirshberg
Hirshberg Publishing, Inc.
11110 Ohio Avenue, Suite 104
Los Angeles, CA 90025
(213) 473-7223
FAX: (213) 312-1773

HIRSHBERG PUBLISHING, INC.
11110 Ohio Avenue, Suite 104
Los Angeles, CA 90025

Printed in the United States of America

Library of Congress Catalog Card Number: 90-71078

ISBN 0-9626928-7-5

This Book is dedicated to the memory of Malcom Forbes
who loved America and helped make her what she is.
May you always be—in the wind.

FOREWORD

By Tim Forbes

Pop loved bikes and biking. As he said to *Playboy* magazine, "Travelling on a bike is invariably a delight. I love the exposure to the elements, being part of them instead of boxed off from them, the way you are in a car. It heightens every one of your senses. Your vision is better. Your concentration is better. You're taking more in every moment. It's terrifically invigorating."

He started riding relatively later in life, at age forty-eight, and spent the next twenty-two years making up for lost time. He rode whenever he could, wherever he could: into the office and out to dinner, on Sunday poker runs and international Friendship Tours. His beloved Harleys took him across China and Russia, Egypt and Pakistan, Thailand, Malaysia and Japan, through most of the countries of Europe and nearly every state in America. Like the postman, he was undeterred by weather of any sort. He rode in rain, sleet and, on occasion, snow. Once I even accompanied him through a blinding, biting sandstorm in the Sinai Desert. He had his share of painful spills, including one that resulted in three broken ribs, a concussion, and a collapsed lung, but he never for a minute considered giving up riding. When friends or reporters would ask about the dangers of motorcycles, Pop would reply, "Sure, motorcycling has risks. If you're hit, it's more likely to hurt than if you're sealed up in a car. But you know that, so all your senses are more alert. You can't

go through life insulating yourself from danger. Everything is dangerous. Living is dangerous. Eventually, everybody dies of it."

Pop enjoyed collecting motorcycles almost as much as riding them, and his stable covers the full gamut of today's best mounts. There are fully loaded touring machines from Honda and Yamaha, pure sport bikes from Japan, including outrageous hot rods like the Yamaha V-max, sport tourers embodied by the BMW R- and K-series bikes, and exotics like the Italian Bimota, the Vetter Mystery Ship, to Brazilian Amazonas and the German Munch. But the centerpiece of the collection and Pop's favorites were the mouth-watering array of Harley-Davidson's finest. He explained his passion for Harleys this way: "Motorcycles are like racehorses. You want to have the best bloodlines, and that means to have a Harley, if you can. It's the most sought after motorcycle in the world, not just here, but in Japan, Europe, all around the globe."

So, as Pop urged his family and everyone else, "Venture out. Adventure. You'll live longer if your spirit's stirred by the world about you. Don't be a shut-in when there's America the Beautiful to see from sea to shining sea. Don't stay put when you can put foot into any part of this still whole, wide, and mostly wonderful world." Best of all, do it on a bike.

CONTENTS

ACKNOWLEDGMENTS

It would not be feasible to attempt to thank each one of the people who gave some help to the author, so I will limit my acknowledgments to the people who were instrumental in helping me go from an idea to the finished product.

First I want to thank Dan Poynter whose book, *The Self Publishing Manual,* was my guide into a world I knew nothing about. Also, for all the times Dan was there for me to answer my questions and to advise me, I will be forever grateful for all his guidance.

To my wife Susan, who put up with all the sixteen-hour days I spent on this project, and for all the lost weekends I spent photographing people. Most of all for coming up with the concept for the cover of this book and also for her story, *A Non Rider's Perspective.*

James Farrell, our cover designer, who under a tight deadline did the impossible and laid out this book, and for taking my wife's concept of a possible cover and perfecting it and giving it life. Jim's contribution has been enormous.

Will Cormier, who illustrated this cover and gave our dream its finishing touches.

Courtney Caldwell, of *American Woman Road Riding Magazine,* who provided me with many important contacts that enabled this project to go smoothly.

Judith Lazarus, for editing this project.

Tom's Camera and Lab, for all his assistance.

And special thanks to Gary Davis, who introduced the author's project to Mr. Forbes' son Tim, who thus provided us with his thoughts on his father.

Chad McQueen, for sharing memories of his father with us.

Sarah Faraday, for her insights into women and motorcycles.

Keith Ball, for his story, *The Question of Brotherhood.* It has given me new insights into motorcycling.

Wayne Thomas, for taking the time for his informative article on the issue of helmet laws.

Larry Grodsky, for his contribution and the benefit of his knowledge in his story, *Experience Speaks.*

Special thanks to Casey Weyandt, the eleven-year-old boy in the photo titled *The Future.*

Also the following people who were instrumental in providing me important contacts and much needed help.

Gary Weyandt

Herb Nanis

Kenny Lumbino

Angelo Anastasio

Patricia Roseman

Benito "Beni" Fabre

Blaire AAronson

My thanks to Ron and Agi Hirshberg, who embraced my dream and believed in me, and whose financial backing made this book a reality.

And lastly to my mom, who has always believed in me and holds a special place in my heart—I love you Rosie.

My personal thanks to everyone in this book who has given it life by their participation. It is because of you that this book lives.

INTRODUCTION

Motorcycling is a total life wish, contrary to the mistaken opinion of many non-riders. The riders you'll meet on these pages will tell you that motorcycling helps them in so many ways. When things are just getting to you, when you need to get away, need to clear your head...it's medicine.

As I interviewed Harley-Davidson riders from all over the country, and even some from other countries, I had three questions in mind: What do you think about when you ride to make it safe? Why do you ride? And why do you ride a Harley-Davidson?

"When I don't ride, everything else suffers." That's what Lorenzo Lamas replied, and I think he said something all of us would have said, because that's it exactly. That's what it is for me.

I need to get out there in the wind and feel it ripping through my hair, feel the sensation of the bike underneath me. To feel and smell and be part of the experience, to have all my nerve endings electrified, and just to feel so totally alive.

I know I can get on my motorcycle for a ride up the coast, say to Monterey, California, spend the night and come back the next day, and feel like I've been gone for a month. It does that much for the soul. I only wish all the non-riders in the world would give themselves at least the benefit of a motorcycle safety course just to experience what motorcycling is; I think we'd have a lot fewer psychiatrists out there if everyone did. It's the best therapy ever invented.

Also contrary to the myth, motorcycling is a very responsible sport. I mean, there isn't a lot of room for error, so you'd better be paying attention. As you go page by page, you'll see that these riders hold a wide variety of successful, responsible careers. When they ride, they carry this responsibility onto the street. They are very safety-oriented and responsible, not only to themselves but to the non-riding public as well. They have the life wish.

I created this book because I don't think it's inconceivable that maybe in ten or fifteen years non-riders might try through legislation to get us off the roads due to misinformation or misperceptions about our sport. I thought that by getting a look at the people they see every day on your streets and freeways, they might understand, perhaps to their surprise, that there are many wonderful people in motorcycling... maybe some of the "bad boy" image is unfounded. Maybe we can all understand each other and our needs a little better, and have respect for each other—the non-riding and riding public together.

Motorcycling really changed my life. When I first got into it, I found myself daydreaming all the time about biking and the romance which is involved, especially when you're out there by yourself and your mind is running wild. I guess I could go on record as saying I never did anything creative prior to getting into motorcycling. I'm sure I had some thoughts, but I just never entertained the fact that I could do anything other than "work" for a living.

Through motorcycling a systematic set of events happened. I conceived a screenplay and collaborated with two writers on a movie about a man getting along in years who finds himself reassessing his life, leaving behind all the things he thought were necessary to function. He goes out on the open road on a motorcycle, experiences new adventures, and winds up finding himself. Then I found myself painting, something else I had never done before. Both of these things seemed so natural to me. And now I find myself writing, self-publishing, and photographing this book. I didn't think of myself as a writer, and surely not a photographer nor a publisher. Somehow, I became all three.

I photographed these people with no extensive technical knowledge, but when I looked through the lens I looked through the eyes of love, like that old story where the man says, "If you could see her through my eyes...." I feel I was able to capture their spirit and portray the subjects the way I wanted to see them.

Much of the success of this project is attributable to the people you are about to meet. Hopefully you will get some insight into why we ride, and why we have this obsession with Harley-Davidson motorcycles. May all of you always ride free, and may you always be in the wind.

THE IRON STALLION

HARLEY-DAVIDSON

CLIFF ALSBERG

44. Florida. TV executive; president of Beth Ohr Congregation. Riding 26 years. 1988 Heritage.

Riding a motorcycle has made me a better car driver. I am really aware of a lot more, now that I'm involved in motorcycling. I guess the main thing is to watch out for the other guy. Also, I won't do anything to alarm my passenger. I ride with great respect for my machine and the cars around me. In a nutshell, I am a very conservative rider.

I think riding is one of the last ways you can feel free and really express your individuality. You know, it's a Walter Mitty kind of lifestyle. You feel part of something very special.

I've got a thing about buying American. I own five cars, and they're all American-made. Three Corvettes and two Cadillacs and my Harley. My Cadillacs are fat and decadent, and there's something about Corvettes; they're macho and impractical and loud. Harley is the same thing. For the last eighty-eight years or so, it's been one of the Hallmark signatures of American machismo, and they can take everything else away. They can buy Columbia Pictures, and they can go out and purchase Rockefeller Center, but Harley is always going to be American, and I just like to own American steel. By the way, I feel that this bike I own is the one Elvis should have had.

MAIKO SARAVIA

37. Uruguay. Custom floor contractor; restauranteur; Harley mechanic for close friends. Riding 26 years.
1989 Springer and 1989 FXST.

To keep in one piece while I ride, I quit drinking some time back. You just cannot handle one of these machines with any alcohol in you. Also, you have to ride according to the traffic situation. There are times when twenty-five miles an hour might be too fast, and other times when fifty-five mph is perfectly safe. You just have to use common sense.

If you have a problem, you get on your motorcycle and somehow it all seems okay. You get a healing from it. You come back with a different face on. Plus, I enjoy my friendships around motorcycling. You know, you buy a

Harley and all of a sudden your base of friendship has grown tenfold. You never pass another Harley rider in distress and not stop for him. This brotherhood makes it so good for me. I love the bond that we all have.

I started racing with a friend in my country on Japanese bikes. Then, people who could afford to sponsor us wanted to race a Harley and saw we were capable of winning races. So, I got into racing Harleys professionally, and I've never quit. I guess you could say I'm hooked.

GRADY PFEIFFER

51. Minnesota. Sales director for electronic component manufacturer. Riding 41 years. 1986 FXRC, heavily modified.

My riding style varies according to the conditions and where I am, but the thing that never changes is that I'm totally alert and concentrating at all times. I never tailgate, and when I am in back of an automobile I ride in his left tire track so I know I'm visible in his rearview mirror.

I ride to get rid of the cobwebs that are there because of the daily grind or the pressures of work. The bike fixes all that for me.

Harley is apple pie and motherhood and the American flag. I feel very patriotic and I like riding American iron. I've wanted one of these things since I was a young kid. Recently, I bought a new 1990 Ultra Classic to ride to Sturgis. Harley-Davidson is the only motorcycle I would consider owning.

GEORGE DRINKHALL • CINDY O'HARA

George: 45. Pennsylvania. Truck driver. Riding 25 years. 1959 Sportster, Model K.
Cindy: 29. California. Hairdresser.

GEORGE: I never ride with the thought that I'm going to get hurt. I rely on my instincts and a positive attitude. There's one thing I insist on having on my bike, and that's a set of loud pipes so everyone around me knows I'm there. That one simple little act has done much to keep me out of harm's way, because if they can't see you, maybe they can hear you. Really, the key to the whole thing is to be one step ahead of everyone else on the road. You have to drive a motorcycle anticipating everything; with that attitude, you will have a successful ride.

I put my gear on, or better yet my chaps, and I feel invincible, like a warrior from another time. What we all represent is freedom. It's too bad that non-riders don't take a month off and somehow experience this . . . I think we'd all be in a better way. To me, a biker on a Harley is a masculine man and the bike is an extension of that. For the people who don't

ride, who get caught up in the pressures of life, therapy might be painting, or an hour with a psychologist somewhere, or maybe some sexual thing behind a closed door, but we get our therapy in front of the whole world, in the wind.

Why Harley-Davidson? It's obvious. It's dependable, and you can customize and create dozens of looks around one frame and one engine. Also, maybe the biggest thing, it's an American product and that does something for me.

CINDY: I love sharing the wind with my man. It's also a real social thing with us, as several of our friends ride, also. Maybe one of the highlights of it all is when we participate in some of the big runs to raise money for muscular dystrophy, and also the Toy Run for children during the Christmas season.

THE IRON STALLION

HARLEY-DAVIDSON

CELEBRITY INTERVIEW

LORENZO LAMAS

*32. California. Actor. Riding 15 years. Chopper, 1955 frame, 1963 engine, outside oiler heads,
1989 Springer front end, restored by Lorenzo.*

In my opinion, you have to ride with the thought that no one sees you. In other words, just consider yourself invisible to other people. When I ride, I keep moving around and trying to stay out of people's blind spots. If you can stay away from cars, you can stay out of trouble. They're the enemy. I think riding an American-made motorcycle is a plus because they're loud and people can hear you. Anything you can do to increase your safety factor should be a priority. Riding is a very serious sport that should be approached with the utmost respect.

When I don't ride, then everything else in my life is affected; my work, my marriage, and my own personal happiness. It's more of what riding helps me continue to do, rather than what it does for me.

Harley is quality to me. This bike and some of the components on it are over twenty-five years old. But with a little spit and polish, it's like brand new. A Harley will last forever if you take care of it. In life you look for longevity, whether in relationships or work, and I find the only motorcycle that has that for me is Harley-Davidson.

CHARLES REDFOOT

58. New Jersey. Exporter/importer. Riding 42 years. 1980 FLH.

I'm very cautious. Fifty-five miles per hour is fast enough for me. It appears that for every mile I do over fifty-five, I have less time to react, so I'm really comfortable holding down my speed. I never drink alcohol or touch a drug of any kind, because these things are poison to a person on a motorcycle. Also, I am never in a hurry. That only causes you to take chances, and there are no percentages in that. And, my last rule is, I pray to my higher power every day to protect me.

My grandfather taught me how to ride horses when I was six years old. I'm a Oglala Indian, an offshoot of the Sioux Tribe, and riding a motorcycle is the closest thing to being free on a magnificent horse, with the sun and the wind to touch your spirit.

Harley-Davidson is not only a motorcycle, it's a tradition and a way of life. I've had mine hand painted with scenes of my Indian culture, and I ride with a medicine pouch on my belt. My two loves are my Indian heritage and my Harley-Davidson, both of them make my spirit soar.

GARY WEYANDT

37. Ohio. Custom bike builder. Riding 27 years. 1988 Heritage.

I ride every single day in all kinds of conditions, and many times I've been caught in heavy rain as my bike, by choice, was my sole form of transportation. I guess the key to keeping the right side up is paying attention to the smallest details—cars leaving driveways, or that turn of the head by the person in the automobile just in front of you. You must ask yourself, "What will he do?" It's total anticipation. One thing I never focus on is the possibility of getting hurt. That only leaves you second-guessing yourself.

I ride to keep myself feeling good about life. It clears my head and rejuvenates me. It's an internal healing.

If you've got to ask me why I'm riding a Harley-Davidson, then all the explaining in the world would not make you understand.

ROGER LINDSKOG

52. Massachusetts. Self-employed. Riding 27 years. 1989 FXR.

"Pay attention" is the best advice I can give anyone. Also, don't drink while you ride or they'll be picking you up off the street. You have to drive very defensively on a motorcycle. I have been riding for twenty-seven years and I've never been down. I ride with the attitude that I'm going to be okay if I apply myself 100 percent to the moment.

You can't explain riding—it's so good, it's unexplainable. I started out with an old, chopper Harley, and through the years it's always been Harleys. They just get into your blood and you're hooked forever. I guess it's the image and the sound . . . there's nothing like that sound.

JOHN COVINGTON

29. California. Restaurant designer. Riding 3 years. 1985 Wide Glide.

It's simple—just figure everyone is out to kill you. Obviously, you want to stay alive. If you ride around with that thought in mind, you'll be riding safely. The bottom line is this: never let your guard down when you're on your machine and you'll be way ahead of the game.

I ride for the joy of it. It's an incredible release. I haven't found anything else in life that comes close to what motorcycling gives me. I don't think that anyone can put into words what riding a bike does for the human spirit.

I only own American. The automobile I drive is American, and my motorcycle is American. Harley-Davidson is a great institution and I'm proud to own one.

JOE TERESI

49. Minnesota. Publisher, Easy Rider magazine, In the Wind magazine, three other publications. Riding 41 years. 1981 Sturgis.

I would say that the first year of riding is the shakiest. You're unsure of yourself and you have no hands-on experience. After a few years of riding, you should be able to deal with any situation. If you're paying attention and sober, there's no reason ever to hit the street. Just don't screw around on a motorcycle. Respect it and you'll be okay. I never think about how to ride and stay safe because it's ingrained and natural to me now, and has been for many years. I guess I could sum it up by saying, "Don't push the corners or your braking capacities or your equipment."

You ask why I ride? Doesn't that go back to the saying, "If you have to ask, you wouldn't understand it"?

I don't think there is anything that feels or sounds like a Harley. I don't like to ride in a group of high-revving motorcycles—it sounds like a swarm of bees; it drives me nuts. The only sound that's soothing to me is that big V-twin. Personally it's only Harley, and I'll tell you something else: I have never sold one and lost money, and I've had plenty of them.

TONY PARSEN • JO JO PARSEN

*Tony: 47. New Mexico. Owner of Tony's Brakes & Alignments. Riding 36 years. 1967 Pan Shovel.
Jo Jo: 3. Riding a modified Indian motorcycle from Italy to look like Grandpa's Harley.
The bike's name is Hardly Harley.*

Basically it's simple: don't hotdog around on your machine, absolutely no drinking, and watch for every little nothing that could become a danger. I'm riding thirty-six years, and at eleven years old, I started on an Indian motorcycle. You learn right away that you cannot win against automobiles, so drive your bike with respect and in a manner that keeps you ahead of it all.

I enjoy riding so much, it's in my blood. I've been across country and through the Southwest on my bike. Once in a while I get the urge and take off for a month or two and just travel. I'll tell you something that is probably unique to how

I acquired my first motorcycle—I traded a bunch of chickens for it. I was so small that someone had to be there when I decided to stop, because I couldn't reach the ground. This year I'm heading out to Sturgis, which I've done many times, and I'm taking the long way.

Harley is the only machine to ride. If they didn't have Harleys, I'd be on an Indian as a second choice. All my life I've been on the best. My grandson is already riding a motorized two-wheel bike, and I can tell by his interest that Harley has another rider to continue the tradition.

WAYNE THOMAS

*43. California. Owner/Creative director of design and marketing firm, co-director of
the California Motorcyclist Association (CMA). Riding 31 years. 1987 Softtail Custom.*

My position, with the CMA, allows me access to an incredible bank of knowledge regarding motorcycle accidents and related safety and training issues, so my approach to riding safely is tempered by it. I can't emphasize enough the value of motorcycle safety courses for all riders, but especially for the beginning rider (about ninety percent of all motorcycle accident and fatality victims have had no formal training). I ride in a constant state of vigilance, continually scanning traffic and watching out for possible intersecting traffic. I use my horn a lot to make sure people approaching from the side know I'm there. I always ride with my lights on, flash my lights at opposing traffic in intersections, and look left-right-left at all intersections, even if I have the light or the right-of-way (as about half of all accidents involve an impact from the left at approximately the 11 o'clock position to the motorcyclist, and a total of seventy-five percent occur in the 11 o'clock to 1 o'clock position). Just these few safety tips, if followed, probably decrease the odds of ever having an accident by a factor of ten to one, or even greater, as your experience level increases.

Riding for me is primarily a form of relaxation. My work and political activities in motorcycling generate a lot of tension and pressure. After five minutes on the bike, however, I can forget about work and become totally absorbed in the unique experience of riding.

Even before I started riding I always wanted a Harley. It was my first image of a real bike and nothing else quite had the sound, feel or look of a Harley and probably never will.

FERD SEBASTIAN

56. Texas. Producer. Riding 35 years. 1987 FLHS.

I ride always anticipating what the cars around me could possibly do to affect me. I always keep a distance between myself and any automobile. Something for me that is a major "don't do" is *don't* ever ride alongside of a truck, or for that matter, an automobile. They'll change lanes and take you out in an instant. I guess the secret really is so simple; stay away from cars and you'll be okay.

I ride my bike at least eighty percent of the time, even to commute to our other home in Lake Tahoe. For me this is the ultimate form of relaxation. I've been riding for thirty-five years and I still get excited about hitting the road on my bike.

Harley-Davidson is the only real motorcycle made, not only in this country, but in the world.

BRUCE RADFORD

40. California. Athletic instructor. Riding 25 years. 1979 FXE.

I ride my motorcycle aggressively. You can't let drivers dictate how you're going to handle traffic situations. You have to take control and make instant decisions. I try to stay in front of automobiles and trucks, and especially anything I can't see around, like a van. You can't ride passively and expect to be trouble free. You have to have a certain aggressiveness to keep you ahead of it all.

Riding, for me, is therapy. I listen to the sound of my motor and it relaxes me. Then there's the brotherhood of riding with your friends. There's nothing better.

What is Harley-Davidson? Well, it's a trip up the coast, almost in a time warp, camping out on the beach with your best friend; it's 1950 and simpler times.

BOB TOLLER • RITA SCOTT

Bob: 36. Arizona. Bob's Cycle Supply. Riding 23 years. Personally owns more than 100 motorcycles; has clients all over the world.
Rita: 29. Court reporter.

BOB: I drive defensively, and I feel that anyone with common sense can learn to ride and not get hurt. I hear stories about guys who get into a wreck every two or three years, and I've got to wonder about that. What are they doing wrong? It's an enjoyable sport if you treat it with respect. You ride long enough and you can handle any situation. But if you're going to ride and show off, then you're destined for problems.

I think everyone can agree that riding relieves stress, and it's a medicine of sorts. You know, you ride down the road and you get to smell the trees and the grass and see life at a slower pace. It just makes you happy. The thing is, when you ride a bike the senses you never seem to use come into play and you become more aware of everything.

When I was sixteen, I used to ride a Japanese bike and I would pull up to a light and smoke those Harleys, and I'd look back and say, "Why would anybody want to ride an old, slow Harley?" Now I understand. You can pass them, but you can't outclass them. I'm older now and cruising is all I'm interested in. I have no desire to race around. My favorite bike in my collection is a 1952 panhead that I bought from an old guy with 10,000 original miles on it, and it hadn't been lit up in twenty years. I changed the oil and plugs, put gas in it, and it fired on the fourth kick. That bike is so original that only the air in the tires isn't factory. I'd rather ride a $500, old, smoking Harley than ride anything else made.

RITA: The wind and the open space you experience make it great to be part of motorcycling. When I first got around bikes, I didn't know one from the other. Now, one can go down the road and I'll tell you what year and model it is. Harleys are addicting and wonderful.

SHERMAN WILLIAMS

30. Tennessee. Production designer. Riding 3 years. Personal bike, heavily modified Sportster.
Photographed with a 1989 Springer.

Be defensive and anticipate your moves 100 percent of the time. You've got to stay alert and have total concentration. You really have to watch out for the other guy and just assume he won't do the same for you. That way you'll be that much more prepared if something unexpected happens. Of course it goes without saying that staying drug free and sober is a must.

I lived in Manhattan before moving to California, and it just wasn't realistic for me to buy a bike in the city. Maybe it was all part of moving to California, but as soon as I moved here, I cut off all my hair and bought a Harley. I guess you could say I fell right into the California life-style.

You ask me why Harley-Davidson? Do I really need to answer that question?

TONY STEWART • CANDICE STEWART

Tony: 41. Canada. Builder. Riding 27 years. 1937 Knucklehead.
Candice: 9. Student.

TONY: My bike is equipped with a suicide shift. It requires so much concentration and coordination just to drive this machine because of the limited amount of technology that was built into this bike in 1937, that all I can think about is what I am doing. I'm not out there in a fog. This bike requires me to drive it with one hand when I'm shifting. I've got to pay attention because obviously in traffic I'm at a disadvantage. This bike keeps me honest. I drive like everyone else is blind. Not that they are, but I know that there's at least one out there that I want to be ready for.

I guess I was born to ride. I started at a young age, and even though the careers I've had in my life would lead some-one to believe that motorcycle riding wouldn't fit in, I have managed to always be on a bike. I've spent years on a commercial icebreaker, and I've also been a farmer. But, no matter what I've done, I've always been a biker.

Harley is the first bike I ever rode and I've never known anything else . . . is there anything else?

CANDICE: What does she like about riding? The driver. She likes being with her dad!

ERNEST BARNHARDT aka "The Mayor"

57. Canada. Semi-retired. Riding 15 years. 1989 Lowrider.

I always try to stay within the law when I'm riding my motorcycle. Speeding doesn't mix with riding a motorcycle. When I change lanes, I turn my head instead of relying on my mirrors, and I use my signals so that automobiles have every chance to know what I am about to do. I sold my last motorcycle when my oldest boy turned sixteen, so he wouldn't be like his dad and be out there riding around on one of these, but I'm wise enough to know you cannot isolate yourself from the experiences of life just to play it safe. Now, he and I both ride together, and I've instilled in him the responsibility to ride with the correct attitude. Safety is really a state of mind.

Riding, to me, is a lot like skiing: you get that feeling of freedom, the air and the wind. You can't get this feeling in the most exotic car, but I can get it on my Harley. As far as I'm concerned, it doesn't get any better than this.

Being on a Harley-Davidson is almost a little like being on the edge of what's perceived as being acceptable, and I think that's part of the thrill of the machine. This Harley has changed my life for the better.

THE IRON STALLION

HARLEY-DAVIDSON

CELEBRITY INTERVIEW

ROBERT DAVI

36. New York. Actor. Riding 21 years. 1979 FLH.

I don't approach riding like a dangerous sport, I approach it cautiously and with great respect. I do not race around on my machine. Life has its own surprises, but I treat my riding so that there are no surprises that I'm unprepared for. I don't try to impress anyone on my bike, and I watch out for the other guy. Basically, it's that simple.

It's a sense of freedom similar to what my acting represents to me. It's not just a profession, it's part of who I am, and this is true of my bike. It's part of me. This experience is absolutely as close as it gets to the Wild West.

I grew up around Harleys. This is the machine that makes it happen for me. It's steel and there is an honesty to this motorcycle.

MOE KORY

47. Israel. Restauranteur. Riding 8 years. 1986 Heritage.

My big thing is that I'm constantly watching for people who like to tailgate, because it only takes one little tap and a whole world of problems open up. My eyes and ears are always looking and listening for potential danger. You must never stray for a moment. Your senses must be 100 percent to produce a safe and enjoyable ride.

It's a tremendous release from the daily grind of business and dealing with people. When I get on my bike, I become part machine, clicking away without emotion. It feels so good to experience the rhythm of the engine.

I own a Harley because it is the best machine built. They are really timeless. It doesn't matter what year bike you own, they're all equally beautiful. Also, it's American, and that's very important to me.

EDDIE "BONES" REYNOLDS

45. California. Crusader for motorcycle freedom. Riding 28 years. 1983 FXST.

Go slow, be satisfied with what they let you have, don't push it. Young people are riding for the thrill and for the speed, but I ride for the wind and the peace it gives me. Just stay totally aware and you'll be able to survive on the street. Don't push your equipment or yourself—there is no room for error.

I don't know if I can explain it, but my grandfather said to me when I was a young boy, don't ever be without a horse. Well, I got my horse, but it's made of steel. In many ways I'm like a cowboy, because when I go somewhere I put my saddlebags and my bedroll on my bike. I pack some food just like a cowboy would. I guess you could say I'm more cowboy than biker. This is the wildest primitive experience you can have in a civilized society.

My Harley, well, I live on it. It's part of my soul, we're one. Harley-Davidson is what America is all about.

FRANK MADDEN

39. New Jersey. Owns Color I, largest painting contractor in Las Vegas, Nevada. Riding 1 year. 1989 Springer.

The thing for me that really made sense when I started riding was taking the National Motorcycle Safety Course. I had ridden years ago when I was younger, but I felt totally unprepared to handle a machine this large without the correct training. That course has made me totally aware of the other people around me, whether it's another motorcycle or a car. It's really helped me understand how to ride safely and with confidence. It's really crazy out there, and without the proper knowledge, you're just shooting the dice.

I ride because that feeling of not being confined is almost mystical for me, and I look forward to the times I have alone with my thoughts and my Harley.

This machine has become a passion in my life, and I have taken several trips out of state in the short time I've been riding. My wish is that everyone could experience a Harley-Davidson. It can definitely be life-altering in a most positive way. It helps you slow down and really take time to experience the simple things.

NINA KENT

27. California. Record company promotions. Riding 5 years. 1989 Sportster.

When I ride, I imagine that everyone is crazy out there. And I visualize that they don't know how to drive, so I have to be that much more alert. I ride covering my brake, so if need be I can react quickly to the unexpected. I think Los Angeles is a hard area to ride in because everyone is in so much of a rush, and our congestion magnifies that. People are crazy in their cars. I drive defensively at all times because I want to enjoy this sport for the rest of my life.

I ride because I love the experience of being free. I've been around motorcycles for twelve years, although I personally have only been riding for five years, so I guess it's fair to say

it is a major part of my life. I'll get on my bike and ride from Los Angeles to San Francisco just as soon as I would go down to the corner to buy a paper. I don't consider riding a few hundred miles in one direction to be a burden. If anything, it is total pleasure.

Harley is American made, and I support the concept. My favorite car is a '67 Mustang—I'm patriotic toward American products. Harley's got class. I like the fact that you can see the engine and it's not covered by yellow and pink fiberglass. It is a beautiful machine, and my bike is my best friend.

JOHN TUCKER

36. California. Contractor. Riding 20 years. 1969 FLH.

I ride assuming that no one sees me. This way I don't expect anything from the cars but the unexpected. It's a war out there, and your ammunition is to be totally aware and alert. Practice your riding skills, and get yourself comfortable with your machine.

I ride for the control I feel on this machine, the power that's in my hands, and the total freedom that motorcycling gives me.

Harleys turn people's heads. You're on a Harley and you become the center of everyone's interest. There's hardly a time I've pulled up to a traffic light when the people in the automobiles around me aren't trying to take a look at my machine. My bike is twenty-one years old and it is really timeless. The whole thought of riding and owning something of such great quality is exciting to me.

DANNY BACEDA • VIRGINIA CAMERENA

Danny: 47. Canada. International banker. Riding 14 years. 1983 Special Construction. 1976 Shovel Head.
Virginia: 46. Arizona. Real estate.

DANNY: When I'm riding this bike, the rule is pay attention to everything, and I mean everything. Riding a bike is strictly a matter of driving for every car around you. You'd better be able to figure out all the variables before they happen. You have to realize you're sitting on a very powerful machine and you have to ride it with respect or it will bite you, and hard.

In Canada I owned many nightclubs which featured celebrities like Sammy Davis and Tony Bennett. With that kind of life, I thought I knew what excitement was. I was wrong. Someone introduced me to Harley-Davidsons fourteen years ago and then I really found out what excitement

was. I ride because it is the most incredible expression of freedom I've ever experienced.

If you're going to own an exciting, exotic car, then it has to be a Ferrari. If you're going to own an exciting, magnificent motorcycle, it has to be a Harley-Davidson.

VIRGINIA: Well, I guess I ride for all the same reasons you've heard from other people, but maybe one you haven't heard is that my man is Italian—I'm not letting this guy out of my sight on this wild-looking motorcycle. That could be the best reason for riding.

BILL McDONALD

46. Texas. Los Angeles County Deputy Sheriff. Riding 20 years. 1989 Heritage.

I think about everything around me. There's really no time to daydream on one of these machines. I ride with a Harley owners group chapter, and safety is a major part of that organization. We all want to get to do this again. With the group we have a road captain and a couple of riding masters that set up the rules for the trip. One of the things that we always do: if a rider breaks down, we all stop until we get him going again. The brotherhood part of Harley-Davidson is something that's near and dear to me.

There's nothing like riding. It's a love of freedom, and if I have problems at home and they appear to be overwhelming, I'll go out and fire up my bike, get on it and go for a ride, and somehow it all gets better.

I love my machine. Before I bought it, I looked at several bikes that copied the Harley look, but I knew I couldn't live with an imitation. I said to myself, "I have got to have the real thing," and I love this bike.

RIC MEAD

53. California. Retired. Riding 42 years. 1984 FXST.

My main rule is to watch out for everyone else. I know where I'm going and I hope they know where they're going. Also, you have to drive within your limits and not get insane on your scooter. You really have to drive with eyes in the back of your head. You have to be aware of everything to stay alive.

I ride for the sheer pleasure of enjoyment. I started on a motorcycle at eleven years old. This is in my blood, and everyone who knows me is aware of how strongly I associate with the motorcycle life-style. I'm also involved in the organi-zation of several runs in California; one that I have a soft spot for is the Toy Run. On our last Toy Run, we riders actually delivered the toys to the children, and that's very gratifying to me personally. My reward is seeing these small children light up with joy because of this simple token of love.

I'm an American and I fought for my country in Korea, and for me, there are no options. I will only own American iron, and part of that reasoning is that there is a tremendous prestige to that. I own several Harley-Davidsons and I wouldn't part with any of them.

ANGELO ANASTASIO • PATRICIA ROSEMAN

Angelo: 38. Italy. Ex-soccer player, New York Cosmos. Entertainment and promotion Adidas worldwide.
Riding 18 years. 1988 Heritage.
Patricia: 28. North Carolina. Model/actress.

ANGELO: I started riding Ducatis up and down the coast of Italy, and by the time I got to college I was on Harleys. My attitude toward riding is totally safety oriented: be defensive and don't daydream. Always look way ahead and read the traffic. Focus on what you're doing; there's no taking chances. Nice and easy keeps you in one piece. When you are riding a $30,000 machine (after several trips to your local customizer) you don't want to scratch it by dropping it; makes sense, doesn't it? I believe in what my gas tank emblem says, "Ride to live and live to ride." That is my motto.

My job is very stressful, and this machine makes that all balance out for me.

Harleys have always been in my life. I love America with a passion, and ride with an American flag on my bike. If Harleys didn't exist, I wouldn't ride. Harley is as American as the eagle.

PATRICIA: The perfect weekend is when the warm, gentle winds are blowing, and Angelo calls me and says, "Let's go for a ride." The wind is rushing through my hair and I'm free from traffic, smog, and congestion of the city. I remember our first bike ride: Angelo showed up with a leather jacket for me and swept me away on a Harley-Davidson. What a way to start a relationship!

TOM REEVES

*41. California. Owner of Classic Cycles; specialty is customizing Harley-Davidsons.
Riding 26 years. Personal bike, 1963 FLH.*

Just don't run over anything sitting on our freeways and you'll be fine. I recently ran over a twelve-foot aluminum ladder. It all came out okay, but I have to comment that my years of experience helped me not to panic. My advice is keep to the speed limit and don't ride in the lane closest to the curb. I've seen many autos back out of driveways right into my path. Don't blast through intersections—give yourself that margin to stop. Also, red lights don't mean a lot with all the people you see trying to run them. I'll tell you something I try never to do, and that's to go out at lunchtime on my motorcycle in the city; too many people trying to cram errands and lunch into sixty minutes, and they're more apt to drive carelessly.

I enjoy riding. Motorcycles are my business. I'm on one everyday. I recently bought a sidecar so my little girl could be with me. I like working on bikes almost as much as riding them.

Harleys are prestige, and they have an incredible resale value. As far as riding one, it's an experience everyone should have.

ROBBIE FINCH

35. California. Carpenter. Riding 20 years. 1980 Shovelhead.

When I'm riding, I totally focus on the cars and their drivers, and if I can possibly make eye contact, I do. I want them to know I'm there and to give me my space, and not just blatantly change lanes or make a left in front of me as if I don't exist. You have to read the drivers' movements when they're behind the wheel for the slightest clue that possibly they are going to do just exactly what you don't want them to. It's really a battle of wits, but it's so much fun doing it.

There's a freedom in motorcycling you can't get anywhere else. You're part of the machine, you become part of the elements . . . it's almost a spiritual experience.

The brotherhood that you can get only in motorcycling is really like entering a special world. People with Harley-Davidsons share a mutual bond, even though they don't know each other. For me, this is really the magic that you get with Harley-Davidson.

ROBERT NATOLI

37. New York. Film technician. Riding 25 years. 1987 Super Glide.

Just cruise and take it easy, and that will go a long way to keep you in one piece. You can't be jamming all the time and expect to stay healthy. I don't speed or show off. Twenty years ago I dumped my bike racing because I was totally doing the wrong thing. For a couple of years there, I didn't ride—I'd get near the bike and have flashbacks. I'm a lot older now and, I like to think, a little wiser. So now I ride with respect for my bike and don't push it anymore. In my youth, I really had a total disregard for the responsibility of riding.

I'll tell you this, I'd sell everything I own before I'd sell my Harley. The only thing that really stops me from riding is pouring rain. Other than that, I'm on this machine every chance I get. I literally ride every day.

I don't know what I can say about Harley-Davidson that hasn't been said already, only that ever since I was a young kid, I've wanted one. I've got one now, and I'm not letting go of it.

CARL JONES

35. California. Clothing designer. Riding 20 years. 1989 Heritage; personal collection, 11 Harley-Davidsons.

I try to ride at a reasonable speed and stay alert. I watch every move that automobile drivers are indicating they'll make. Don't drop your guard for a moment. When you're on one of these things, you have to be 100 percent into the moment. I really enjoy riding with my friends, but even there I like to be in a group of no more than five people who are familiar with each other's riding habits. Sometimes your fellow bikers can make it difficult to feel safe and comfortable because of their lack of experience when it comes to riding in a group.

I ride to forget about work and to relax. I like the feeling of being on a bike and not being confined to an enclosed automobile. You're out there sitting on your motorcycle in the wind, and if that doesn't make you feel free, I don't know what does.

The look of Harley-Davidson—I absolutely love the nostalgic appearance of a Harley. Also, it's American, and that is very important to me. It feels good to ride something made in America.

THE IRON STALLION

HARLEY-DAVIDSON

CELEBRITY INTERVIEW

CHAD MCQUEEN

29. California. Actor. Riding 24 years. 8 motorcycles in his collection; Harleys, Indians, and 1 Triumph.

I started riding at five years old. My dad was in love with motorcycling and instilled that passion in me. To ride this long and stay healthy, you've got to have a good foundation of the principles of riding. I started off dirt biking, and those skills I learned have made me very knowledgeable about riding on the street. I'm 100 percent tuned in when on a bike. Staying alive requires you to be way ahead of everyone else mentally. I don't want to be one of those who says it wasn't my fault. Anticipate, react, and believe in your abilities.

Maybe I have an edge because at nine years old I was racing in the dirt, but everyone is capable of improving his or her riding skills.

I ride because it's a part of me. I really don't know anything else. Motorcycles were part of our family life, and I love the sport with a passion. It is the greatest feeling in the world to be out there on a machine.

I'm pro-American and that's why it's Harley-Davidson and Indian motorcycles for me.

TOBY RADICE

42. New Jersey. Blackjack and roulette dealer in Las Vegas. Riding 28 years. 1989 FXST.

You have to ride with eyes in the back of your head. I never stop at a light that I'm not looking into my mirrors. Drivers are really unconscious about us, and you'd better be riding with that thought every time you fire up that bike. And it should go without saying, you have to be sober. I've spent all these years riding and never have had any problems, and I have to believe that it's all attitude.

I just love to be in the open air and feel the wind on me. It's not transportation to get from here to there, it's really an adventure to harness the power of this motorcycle.

Even as a young boy, I had a fascination with Harley-Davidsons. When I was fourteen years old and living in New Jersey, I bought a Sportster. Not old enough for a license, I rode around in my back yard and fantasized about being out there on the New Jersey Turnpike.

Today, my closest friends all own Harleys, and it's great to get together and talk about bikes and forget about all the other nonsense that wears you down. I feel fortunate that motorcycling has been a part of my life for so long.

BOBBY D'ACCARDI

44. New Jersey. Stone cutter. Riding 25 years. 1989 FLHTC.

I've had a lot of years of safe riding and it really comes down to staying alert and being cautious. It only takes a small effort on a rider's part to keep himself safe. This sport is the best there is if you're responsible about it. I believe you have to be much more cautious than when you're in a 5,000 pound car; there's no room for error.

Riding a motorcycle is like a zen experience. You don't think about anything but the moment. It's the best therapy there is.

When I was a young kid my buddies and I were into Harleys. Today, twenty-five years later, they're still a part of my life.

NICK GUTSUE

50. Michigan. Criminal defense attorney. Riding 37 years. 1982 Wide Glide.

You have to be offensive and defensive at the same time: offensive in the sense that you have to be able to get out of harm's way, and defensive knowing you can see them better than they can see you. You're much more maneuverable than they are. Absolutely never override your equipment—leave yourself a margin of safety, and always leave yourself an out.

I ride for the freedom of movement, and for the freedom of expression.

I'm riding a piece of history. It's the state of the art for the origin of motorcycles. Harleys today are basically not that far removed from the early 1900s. I like the fact that I'm riding history.

RHONDA GUTSUE

24. Wisconsin. 1989 World Go-Cart Champion; involved with the 1990 PPG Indy Car World Series Race Car Team; mother and wife. Riding 8 years. 1985 FLT.

Expect the unexpected. Two-wheel sports such as motorcycling require the utmost respect. In traffic situations, give yourself room on both sides in case you suddenly have to move to avoid danger. And remember, machines require total concentration to be ridden successfully.

Personally, I came to motorcycling through my husband, Nick, and for our wedding he gave me this Harley you see here. We took our honeymoon on it. I love to have the wind running through my hair. I feel free. It actually makes me feel closer to nature.

There's a mystique to Harleys. You get people from all walks of life on these machines. The friendships and good times that have come to us through motorcycling are priceless.

MIKE REDMOND

43. Massachussets. Management and sales of hi-tech computers. Riding 28 years. 1990 FXST.

I'm very defensive. All the years I've been on a bike safely could only have been accomplished by being totally into what I'm doing on that bike. No reckless driving or daydreaming; I'm always prepared for anything. I started out racing dirt bikes; I got into that by accidentally meeting Steve McQueen —he introduced me to that sport. The experience I got racing in the dirt has helped me tremendously on the street. I understand my equipment and what it can and can't do. You spend big dollars for these Harleys and you don't want to drop them.

Eleven years ago when my daughter was born, my wife begged me to quit riding, and also to quit flying airplanes. Then I started having problems in my personal life and she

said, "Mike, what do you need to get right again?" And I said, "I need to be back on that motorcycle in the wind." Now when I get uptight, she tells me, "You know, Mike, you need a ride." And that's probably why I'm still married twenty-two years to the same woman. As a matter of fact, she bought me this motorcycle. It's one of five made by Dudley Perkins in San Francisco.

Why Harley? Well, what else is there? In the dirt, I'll ride a Japanese bike, but I can't understand why anyone would ride anything but a Harley on the street. For cruising, it cannot be beat. It's truly a motorcycle. And something I particularly like, it takes me back to my youth every time I get on it.

MYRON LARRABEE • CINDY FAULKINBURY

Myron: 36. Arizona. Co-owner of World Gym; Gold Coast Body Building Champion. Riding 24 years. 1989 Heritage.
Cindy: 35. Arizona. Co-owner World's Gym. 1989 Miss Arizona. Riding 15 years.

MYRON: Go by the rules of the road and you shouldn't have any problem. You can't hotdog around and expect to be trouble free. Don't drink and ride, and don't do drugs. Those combinations will kill you on a motorcycle.

Riding gives me the freedom I need. I've had a love of riding for many years now and I would say motorcycles will always be part of my life.

The reason I went with Harley-Davidson is because it's American made and I'm an all-American man. Also, the

sound and the feel of Harley can't be beat. Motorcycling is truly in my blood.

CINDY: I like to ride because it gives me a feeling of control. The road is yours when you ride on a bike. Of course, the sound and the feel and the freedom are a big part of Harleys. In fact, in a few days I'll be picking up an FLH that I recently purchased, and I can't wait to bring it home!!

LEO COHEN

48. Minnesota. Retired importer/Distributor. Riding 8 years. 1988 FXST.

I think about how much it would hurt to hit the pavement, and that makes me pay attention. I'm very careful to watch out for people in cars on either side of me, and to constantly watch the road for debris that might cause a problem. I've gone all over the United States on a bike, and Canada. On one trip home from Canada it rained the whole way. I made the trip safely because I believe that by being acutely aware of the changing circumstances when you ride, and by driving accordingly, you can make any trip a safe trip. You just have to realize that sometimes even fifty-five mph is too fast.

I ride to take in and enjoy everything around me, and to feel the wind in my hair and the sun on my face. You will never experience those things in a car.

I can appreciate a fine machine, whatever it is, but with Harley you get a fine machine and a legend.

STEVE BEST

36. California. Co-owner of Van Nuys Harley-Davidson with his sister, Sue Merrit. Riding 25 years. Personal bike, 1969 FLH.
Photographed with a 1990 Low Rider.

I ride as if I'm invisible. That psychology will keep you healthy. I ride with a very mellow attitude—no cutting in between traffic or riding to show off. I'm not a recreational rider. I'm not out there on my bike every day, but I do take major trips that last for three days and maybe a thousand miles. This year I'm going to Sturgis, but for me it will be for the ride and the wind, more than the destination.

It's freedom; it's the love of the machine. I was born with it in me. From a young age, I wanted to ride. I ride for per-

sonal pleasure and not to be seen. For me, it's an individual expression of myself.

There are a lot of imitations out there, but Harley-Davidson cannot be copied. It's the feel and the sound. When you get up on the freeway and you're on the cam, the only way I can describe it is "freight train." It's hard for me to believe this is the only American motorcycle made, but that's what it is, and no one has been able to capture Harley's magic.

MARK SIEGEL

29. California. Professional helicopter pilot. Riding 14 years. 1990 FXSTC.

Like a lot of riders, my approach is to assume every individual is going to come into my path and cause me potential danger. Beyond obeying safety rules like speed limits and lights, a critical point to staying alive on a bike is to see something before it could happen. I clear all intersections before I jam on through. I don't care if the light is green and I have the right of way, I'm looking for the unexpected. I'm suspicious of all left-turning vehicles, and slow way down when I see them. I always leave room to swerve out of the way of an oncoming car. It's just not having the right of way that keeps you alive.

There's nothing like the feeling of being on a Harley by yourself, running down the highway with the wind going through your hair, the ocean on your left and some pine trees on your right. You can't explain riding in words. It needs to be experienced first hand.

I've ridden and owned a lot of motorcycles in fourteen years. But five years ago I rode a Harley for the first time, and after you experience 600 or 700 pounds of iron beneath you going down the highway, you know there's no other machine. There are Cadillacs and Volkswagens, and I'm on a Cadillac.

THE IRON STALLION

HARLEY-DAVIDSON

CELEBRITY INTERVIEW

JACK SCALIA

40. New York. Actor. Riding 22 years. 1987 Heritage.

For starters, I have spent a lifetime in sports, and I've got to believe that athletic ability is an asset when you figure in the reaction time that is sometimes required to keep you out of a tight spot. I have a lot of respect for my bike and for the road, as far as what my limitations are. I drive aggressively but carefully, and don't wait for other people to dictate how I should react to a situation. I just do what has to be done to keep myself safe. Harleys are very heavy bikes, and they're not to be toyed with or driven like a rocket. I don't take chances when it comes to motorcycling; I take this all very seriously.

I ride for the freedom it gives me, the total wonderful sensation of being free. I feel no pressure when I ride; I'm like an eagle; my soul soars, and the connection with the spirit of an eagle is something I relate to very strongly.

The reason I'm on a Harley is that it's American and that's the bottom line. I'm an American, and this bike is bought, paid for and ridden by someone who's proud to own an American legend.

KELLY SNYDER

28. California. Film editor. Riding 1 year. 1982 FLH.

As we all know, it takes total concentration to ride. Here I am on a very heavy motorcycle, but by paying attention and staying in the moment, I can enjoy this sport with confidence. I am constantly looking for situations that could be potential problems, and I avoid them by staying alert. When I get on my bike, I mentally visualize that everything will be okay, and I make a connection with God and thank Him for His protection. I feel I have a wall of safety around me.

I ride now because initially I rode with my boyfriend, and sitting on the back of his bike convinced me to buy my own. I feel that's a good enough reason to ride.

I really have a love affair with Harleys, and as far as I'm concerned, this is rolling art.

SPIKER

34. Michigan. Pastry chef/Chemical dependency unit technician. Riding 10 years. 1986 Modified Sportster.

I go slow. That's my primary thing, to take care of myself. And, of course, riding solo you have much more control of the machine. I just took my rear pegs off, and I think I like not having the responsibility of a passenger. A big thing overlooked by a lot of cyclists is sitting at a light daydreaming. It's really a place where you should be watching for autos approaching from all directions. It can be deadly, even when you're standing still.

I don't know why I ride. I have no idea.

I like the way Harley looks and sounds. My Sportster is slim and fast and lean looking—mine is heavily modified, and this thing really hops.

MIKE STEINBERG

49. New York. Developer of custom homes. Riding 31 years. 1987 FXLR, heavily modified.

Paranoia is healthy on a motorcycle. I watch everything when I'm riding. I just figure they're all out to get me, so that attitude keeps me razor sharp on the road. Always anticipate that someone will do something stupid to affect your safety, and you will be one step ahead of them.

I ride because it gives me great pleasure. When I sell my next home, I'll be buying another Harley. The friendships and the brotherhood are priceless. When I was eighteen, I had a Harley and my best friend Herb Nanis (see page 68) didn't have a bike. I loaned him $175 so he could buy a bike and we could hang out and ride together. It's thirty-one years later, and we're still riding Harleys together.

I ride Harley because it's the feel, it's the sound; there's a toughness to Harley-Davidson. It's a great thrill to ride this machine.

RON HIRSHBERG

47. New York. Manufacturer. Riding 31 years. 1989 Heritage.

I'm always aware of who I'm riding with. Be sure you're riding with people capable of handling their bikes, so they don't become a threat to you. It's more than just watching out for automobiles. I'm very careful. I respect my bike and I ride well within my limits. I'm fully aware of what my machine can and can't do, and I don't take advantage of it.

I don't think anyone can put a finger on why there's this love affair with Harleys. I have enough toys in my life to keep me busy. I was third in the world in offshore racing, but my two speedboats sit in the marina; maybe every two months or so I'll take one out. There is something about the bike that

the minute you leave the driveway, you're beginning your pleasure. It's instant gratification. I think as baseball and football are great common denominators where strangers can meet and start up friendships, so it is with Harleys. There is no one you wouldn't talk to if you were in your leathers and they were in theirs. The motorcycle is a bond and that becomes the brotherhood. You're instantly equal.

Harley-Davidson is Americana and God bless the flag! And if there ever was an American thing to do, it's riding one of these machines.

OLIVER SHOKOUH

44. Michigan. Owner of Glendale Harley-Davidson; coordinator of the Love Ride; major fund-raiser for the Muscular Dystrophy Association. (Last year, raised over $500,000 in one day with the participation of 7,200 motorcycle riders and the grandson of the founders of Harley-Davidson, Willie G, and Malcolm Forbes.) Riding 31 years. Personal bike, 1990 Dresser.

I'm extremely defensive. I always ride within my abilities and I don't get crazy. I never drink when I'm riding my bike; that only gives you false courage, and that brings disaster. There are a lot of crazy people on the roads, and you need to be alert to anticipate and protect yourself from careless drivers. Sometimes you're forced to do their jobs for them, and that's the attitude you'd better have to survive.

Riding is the ultimate feeling of freedom. You can go anywhere on a bike, up any highway or down any side road. You're a lot more maneuverable than in an automobile, and

that feeling is incredible. If you wanted to, you could get one of these things to climb stairs. In the right hands and with proper training, they're amazing. There's a mystique and charisma about Harley-Davidson. I guess part of it is the history. It's just the most exciting motorcycle there is.

When I bought my first Harley I kept it locked up in my garage, and before I went to sleep I used to look in there because it felt like something was alive in my garage. Maybe that will help explain what I feel about a Harley-Davidson.

MIKE ISENBERG

25. Florida. Clothing manufacturer. Riding 10 years. 1988 Sportster.

The rules I have for riding safely are pretty simple: don't drive and drink, and try to avoid night riding, especially if you're alone. That one lone taillight out on the freeway is really not that visible. Of course, if you're with someone else, that helps the situation. The most important thing to remember is to keep the shiny side up and the greasy side down and you will be okay.

I ride for the exhilaration of it. The wind in the hair, being free, letting go; also for the edge. I love the control that is involved.

It's solid, it's American, it's a fixture of the American philosophy. Build it right the first time and it will be around forever.

KENYA JACKSON

52. California. Supervisor for Industrial Janitorial Service. Riding 21 years. 1979 FLH Shovelhead.

I just think about the automobiles in back of me and on either side of me, and I know how vulnerable I am. I consider them the enemy, and I know I'd better not get careless. I've been riding a long time and there's no daredevil stuff for me. You can leave that for Evel Knievel. You have to treat your machine with the utmost respect.

If I didn't have a motorcycle, I don't know what I'd do. I've gotten rid of everything I had in the last twenty years, but I always managed to keep my Harley. There is no way I am ever going to be without my motorcycle. Riding is really in my blood. I don't do much riding around town, but I do take trips on my bike, and I try to use the streets only to get to the freeway; I feel the highway is a lot safer than the city streets.

Harley is the ultimate machine. It's the Rolls Royce of motorcycles. You get yourself a Harley and then you can say you have a motorcycle.

BLAIR AARONSON

34. Maryland. Bond trader/Musician. Riding 1½ years. 1989 Heritage.

I rode motorcycles ten years ago, and for one reason or another, I stopped. When I decided to get back into riding, I knew I had to take a safety course because we live in a very congested city, and how I rode back then wouldn't have left me prepared for current conditions. I can tell you this— what I've learned in the California Motorcycle Safety Course would help anyone to enjoy this sport safely. I'm now planning to take the advanced course. The knowledge that you can acquire translates into many hours of safe driving.

I ride just for the sensations and freedom I experience on my bike. It really frees me from my conservative lifestyle, and in some ways it's almost like my music, because I find myself being very creative mentally when I'm riding.

Why Harley-Davidson? It's not just the bike, it's the lifestyle that goes with it. If I were to live a fantasy life, it would be on a Harley.

JERRY LAWRENCE

45. Canada. Motorcycle police officer in Los Angeles, California; president for last 10 years of Los Angeles Blue Knights. Riding 27 years. 1982 FLT.

I am always driving defensively and I'm always conscious of leaving myself an out. Personally, I believe in wearing a helmet, and that probably goes back to when I started with the police force. Maybe the biggest safety factor is for the motorcycle rider to be conscious of his equipment and keep it trouble free by maintaining the basics—checking your chain and always running with the correct tire pressure; visually checking your bike out before you ride it for anything that might possibly be loose. It's my opinion that motorcycles don't crash, riders do, and so many times we find that their equipment was substandard and not properly maintained. I've ridden between my job and my personal life over a million miles, and I've never dropped one yet. I have to believe that the right attitude, along with good equipment and proper training, is the answer to safely riding a motorcycle.

Currently, I am considered to be the most senior motorcycle officer in the world, and riding is such a source of enjoyment for me that in my free time I'm always on my personal Harley. One could not ask for anything better. These Harley-Davidsons are really a large part of my life, and just recently I went back to Milwaukee and became a certified Harley-Davidson mechanic for the police bikes. To live in Southern California and get paid for riding a motorcycle is a dream come true.

A Harley is a motorcycle. It's got the sound and it has the comfort. It's American made, and I feel it handles better than the Japanese bikes because it has such a low center of gravity. And when it comes to looks, Harley is No. 1.

JULIE ROYER

19. Colorado. Aspiring actress/Model. Riding 1 year. 1989 Sportster.

There's so much that goes into riding safely, but I always try to apply the fundamentals, like signaling to turn, and staying in my rearview mirror. I am very aware of people turning left in front of me. They can look at you, even make eye contact, and then—bang! They shoot out in your path. I use my throttle to let people know I'm there. For me, a loud bike is a lot safer than silently pulling up to an automobile, because it appears to me if they can't hear you, they probably don't know you're there. In effect, my pipes become my horn.

I love to ride. The air, the sound of the bike, the freedom of it all. When I'm feeling down and I get on my bike, it all gets better. It's my escape. I'm in my own little world.

I ride Harleys because they're cool. This bike was a present and I'm crazy about it. Also, the big Harley happenings like the Love Ride and the Toy Run are really a blast for me. The whole thing with Harley, whether it's riding or hanging out with your fellow riders, is a great experience.

ALAN EDWARDS

45. California. Owns Alan Edwards Salons and hair products. Riding 9 years. 1988 Heritage.

All my senses are tuned in to the moment when I'm riding. I'm totally aware of everything that can affect me. I spent several years riding dirt bikes, and I feel that has given me an edge on the street. Outside of the fact that you have to have the fundamentals down and be tuned in to stay safe on a motorcycle, you can't concentrate on getting hurt, or you stand a chance of making it happen. You have to believe in your abilities and be aware that, yes, there can be a danger, but you're going to treat riding responsibly.

Riding gets rid of all the stress in my life. You get out there on the freeway and you feel the speed and the machine beneath you, and it's exhilarating. Also, I enjoy the friendships I share with other people in this sport. You make friends with people that possibly you would never get to know if you didn't have this common denominator.

A Harley-Davidson is like a rolling piece of art; I put it in the same category as anything I own that qualifies as art.

THE IRON STALLION

HARLEY-DAVIDSON

CELEBRITY INTERVIEW

RAY SHARKEY

37. New York. Actor/Producer. Riding 3 years. 1987 Heritage, modified to look like a 1940 Arizona State Police bike.

When I'm on this bike I become part of it. I never remove myself from the situation. I'm 100 percent into the moment. I never think "what if," because then I've taken myself out of the situation and I'm outside of it looking at it, not part of the bike anymore. That means you're open to problems because you're not really there. I've had to learn to stay safe, and I personally feel that riding with a small group or even with another person makes you that much more visible. For a while I was the Joe Montana of motorcycle riding. I had a great offense, but no defense, and group riding taught me a lot about safety. You can learn a lot from your fellow rider. There's no such thing as a yellow-green light for me. It's

green or it's red, and I obey the rules. You know it's us and them, and you have to realize your limitations and vulnerabilities.

When I ride I don't think about anything else except what I'm doing. I feel the rhythm of the engine and it's like a song to me; it keeps me going. This sport actually helps me stay sane. You know, when I ride this bike, I sit in it, not on it. I become part of it.

I'm a product of the '50s and the '60s, and cruising and chrome is really what it's all about for me. It's also American. It's the last traditional male bonding. It's really a brotherhood.

MICHAEL MIKLENDA

41. Czechoslovakia. Custom home developer. Riding 25 years. 1988 Heritage.

It's hard to ride and always be thinking about not getting hurt, but I never focus on the danger. It's there, you know it exists, but you are equipped if you have taken the time with the proper skills to avoid a mishap. I can take care of myself on a motorcycle, but I know that I cannot always predict what the other guy will do, so you just have to ride with total awareness. Look at your surroundings, the weather conditions, the traffic conditions, and ride accordingly. Common sense goes a long way in this sport.

I ride for excitement and for the thrill, and also for the relaxation of it. You get on a different wavelength when you're on a motorcycle, and the stress just disappears.

Harley-Davidson is a form of magic. It has no competition.

VAL GARAY • TRACY SULLIVAN

Val: 40. California. Record producer. Riding 25 years. 1987 FXST.
Tracy: 21. California. Clothing business.

VAL: One of my rules I try to adhere to is don't ride at night—you're not visible enough. Also, stay out of the rain. If you're caught in it, that's one thing; but I feel to go out in it on purpose drives up your chances of making errors, and we all know that when it rains in Los Angeles the freeways are like bumper cars at amusement parks. I never drink and drive. In fact I never do anything and drive. You always have to watch blind intersections, even if you have the right-of-way. I constantly have this image of someone running a red light and turning me into a grease spot. If you keep that fear in your mind, it will pay off. Maybe the biggest thing is, don't daydream: you'll live a lot longer.

There is an element of danger and an element of freedom that you only get riding a Harley. A Japanese bike is high technology and a Harley is an antiquated piece of technology, but it's a wonderful part of Americana that I hope will never go away. Four years ago, I knew everyone who had a Harley from this area. We'd go down to Johnny Rockets and there'd be thirty guys. Now, everytime you look around you see a Harley. It has become something that people want to be part of.

The feelings and sensations you get on a Harley are priceless. This is risk exercise, and this kind of addiction is so good for you.

TRACY: I absolutely love riding, even though my role is as a passenger. Hey, I grew my hair long for this bike. Although it took me a while to find the man with the bike, now I have both.

HERB NANAS

49. New York. Personal manager/TV motion picture producer. Riding 31 years. 1987 FLHS.

As I watched the different cycles of my riding evolve, I find myself riding safer and much more conservatively. I have no desire to speed. I don't ever get on a motorcycle and go somewhere quickly. I cruise, totally conscious of everyone around me. You don't have a chance if you're not.

This sport makes me think about the wholesomeness of life and makes me conscious of the serenity that it brings me. The real pleasure I get is being out away from everything. No city hustle, no phone ringing off the hook. I actually get

regenerated when I'm on my bike. This business I'm in is a twenty-four-hour responsibility to the people I work with and manage. I'm always available for them. Having the bike helps me get back to the basics and clear my head. It's simply an adventure that takes me away from the enormous pressures of my responsibilities.

Harley is a great American tale of a company that had it all and lost it and came back bigger and stronger than ever before. This company is really what America is all about.

DARREN GIARRUSSO

26. California. Owns a trucking business. Riding 21 years. 1989 FXST.

I started with bikes that had motors on them when I was five years old, and I can tell you that I found out very early that speeding on a motorcycle is the thing that will get you into trouble. As a kid, I rode way too fast, and now I know you don't get many chances at tempting fate in this sport. Your reaction time is changed dramatically when you're driving a bike, especially in traffic conditions. My philosophy now is I just cruise and enjoy where I am at the moment. Stay aware and you can ride safely and enjoy this sport forever.

This is absolutely my favorite pastime. I can't put into words how much I love to ride.

I'm one of the fortunate few, because ever since I was old enough to be licensed to drive a motorcycle, I've owned Harley-Davidsons. Owning another brand would never be an option. Once you've experienced a Harley, there are no other motorcycles.

WILLIE SCHEFFER

41. California. Line mechanic for Harley motorcycles; road racer; drag racer. Riding 27 years. XR 1000.

I concentrate on the ride, and that's really the key. If you are there mentally, you'll be okay. If you ride and daydream about your bills or your job or family problems, you might as well stay home because you are riding at a tremendous disadvantage to your safety. Riding motorcycles is a 100 percent mental commitment at all times. It's just like a racetrack— you cannot let off on your concentration.

I ride because it's the best and the safest high there is, when you consider the alternatives.

Harley is a good product. It doesn't go obsolete like other brands. It's a twin, and the best thing about Harley-Davidson is you can customize it to no end.

HOLLISTER WHITWORTH

42. Texas. Actor/Producer. Riding 28 years. 1990 FXST heavily modified; 1 of 7 motorcycles in his collection.

Watch really hard when you ride. Mistakes can be permanent. I ride in small groups with my friends. You can be a lot safer with a small group, say three or four people, than being a lone rider out there on the freeway. You have to ride with a higher degree of awareness about everything that can possible affect your immediate situation.

Riding is something I really love. I started riding at fourteen years old. I would have begun sooner, but my parents wouldn't let me. This is something that is part of who I am. I can say motorcycling is in my blood.

Harley is really the only bike that you can customize to make an individual statement about yourself. I have always been hooked on Harley-Davidsons since I was a kid.

RAFAEL FRANCISCO CARMONA,
aka "CARMEN" • SUSAN CARMONA

Carmen: 47. New York. President, Iron Stallion Productions. Author/Publisher. Riding 4 years. 1984 FXST.
Susan: 36. California. Promotional sales. Artist/Writer, wife and mother.

CARMEN: I do so many things in my mind when I ride that I could be here all day talking about them. I play chess in my mind with the cars—I'm constantly trying to figure out what every auto I approach or have coming at me is going to do. If I overtake a van or a car with body damage, I do it quickly, with enough space between him and me in case he moves into my path suddenly . . . . I figure if he has body damage on his car, he probably spends some amount of time daydreaming. When I ride, I'm in my rearview mirrors as much as I'm looking ahead, so I know if someone is blowing by cars in back of me and getting ready to pass me at a high rate of speed. I always ride with my high beams on in the daytime; you're virtually invisible when your lights are off. A rider and his bike blend right into either the vehicle directly in

back of it or into the surrounding homes, fences, etc., but a rider with his lights on during the day is visible from a great distance. To ride successfully, you almost have to possess a sixth sense. This might seem mystical, but it's more intended to mean that your mind must be totally committed to the moment, and beyond.

Why do I ride? Better yet, how could I survive without riding? I live for the free time I can spend on my machine—that time when I know I'm on my way home, I'm gonna take my Harley out, hear that sound again, and feel the wind beating on me. I look for excuses to go forty miles out of my way to buy a newspaper; a typical weekend day means at least 250 miles of riding.

How do I feel about my Harley-Davidson? This sport and

that motorcycle have led to a world I never knew, and to the fulfillment of dreams I never thought would come true. When I leave my home in the morning, I look into the garage to see if she's alright. I love that machine; it has a life of its own. For me, it's the past—it brings me back to the 1950s, hanging out with my friends on street corners, much simpler times.

No amount of imitation can capture the legend that has survived for almost ninety years. A Harley-Davidson is like a 1952 Cadillac convertible with the top down. You're in a time warp of nostalgia and greatness, and the magic of rolling history.

SUSAN: I can't say it was exactly love at first sight for Harley and me; you see, Harley used to be my rival when it came to my husband's free time on the weekends. When you know better than to challenge loyalties you know things have gotten pretty serious.

So what's a motorcycle widow to do? I don't mind being a passenger but I really don't see my future on the back of a Harley for very long since I enjoy experiencing things firsthand and not behind someone else. Being left behind watching and listening to an open-throttled bike disappearing off into the distant horizon without me isn't much fun either. So, I decided an adjustment needed to be made on priorities. I changed my attitude. I'm getting my own Harley.

I took the California Motorcycle Safety Course and passed with a little more confidence than when I started. It was a valuable and eye-opening experience and very humbling, too, I might add. Bikers make it all look so easy but, believe me, there's a lot going on with the bike and your surroundings at each moment you're on that machine to know it's a sport riders need to take very seriously and be trained for.

I plan on riding at least 3,000 miles before getting the Harley of my dreams, a Heritage. Needless to say, I've gotten my husband's attention!

FRANK LEWIS
62. California. Retired truck driver. Riding 37 years. 1985 FLHTC.

My rules for safe riding are: watch everyone that can affect your safety, especially people in rental cars who are not that familiar with our freeways or with some of the things that we are allowed to do in California, like splitting traffic. On the city streets, I watch for people sitting dead still in parked cars. I can't tell you how many times I've seen people just peel out of a parking space into the flow of traffic. I guess it's fair to say that with all these years of riding I've done, I really practice it with the right frame of mind and with the responsibility that the sport demands.

I enjoy riding because it gives me peace of mind and recharges my batteries. This bike I'm on was bought in October 1985, and currently has 83,000 miles on it. I guess it's fair to say that I love to ride.

Harley-Davidson is the only bike I ever really wanted to ride. All my sons happen to ride Hondas, and I've test driven them when they needed me to, but I'll tell you this, I wouldn't trade my Harley-Davidson for ten Hondas.

MIKE KERSHAW

29. California. Musician. Riding 11 years. 1990 FXST Springer.

Riding safely is watching out for the other guy. I don't speed and I don't get crazy on my bike. I like riding and I want to do this for a long time to come. By taking it easy and being defensive, I know I will be able to enjoy my machines safely.

Riding is very relaxing to me. No matter what kind of week I've had, or for that matter, even if it was only a rough day, I get on my machine and life suddenly looks better. My dad had a 1962 BSA and I can remember sitting on the tank at five years old—my first experience with the wind. I guess I fell in love with motorcycles way back then.

You ask me why Harley-Davidson? I didn't know there was any other bike.

GEORGE DARINGER

27. Spain. Actor/model. Riding 21 years. 1987 Sportster.

If you can ride and pass everyone, you will be okay. What I mean by that is get away from traffic—no traffic, ninety-nine percent of your problems are solved. Sometimes you forget; you feel so comfortable on your bike, you're part of it, and you drop your guard. Hopefully, it will be something that your instincts will take care of. In other words, don't get complacent.

I would love to be able to fly and experience what a bird does, but since I can't, I do my flying on a motorcycle.

Harleys are steel and incredible power, and for me, that represents what a motorcycle is.

THE IRON STALLION

HARLEY-DAVIDSON

STALLION

CELEBRITY INTERVIEW

MIGEL FERRER

35. California. Actor/Writer. Riding 20 years. 1948 Panhead.

I ride like I'm invisible. I used to fly airplanes, and the secret of flying safe is to fly way ahead of the airplane, and this is also true of bikes. You have to examine options and ride way ahead of the motorcycle, at least a block and half ahead of yourself. Examine the body language of the automobile and focus in on what the driver of that car is telegraphing to you—possibly he is not using his signals or brake lights, but is he turning his head as an indication that here comes a U-turn or maybe a lane change? There are so many variables; try to project what that driver is going to do.

I ride because it gives me a feeling I can't get anywhere else in life. I can have a terribly awful day, and within ten minutes after I get on my bike, it's all gone. I ride my Harley instead of psychotherapy. Riding is the most therapeutic thing I do.

Harley-Davidson for me is the only motorcycle in the world, and I've owned them all. This is my third Harley, and it's always going to be Harley-Davidson for me. They're magic.

VICTOR GUEVARA • IRMA NIEVES

Victor: 40. New York. Owns a cellular phone business. Riding 25 years. 1989 Heritage.
Irma: 32. New York. Career woman.

VICTOR: When you are riding, watch for and pay attention to the automobiles that could possibly come into your path and cause problems. You have to be able to project situations and be ready to react if they become a reality. I raced dirt bikes when I was a boy, so a lot of this is instinct for me. On the freeway I ride in the No. 1 lane so I don't have to worry about merging traffic or exiting cars. A whole lot of riding is just common sense. Also, it's obvious that no one should be operating a machine with alcohol in them.

I ride for the love of the sport and the feel of the machine, that power in your hands. Also, there's nothing like the com-

bination of a Harley-Davidson and a woman sitting in back holding on to you.

Harley is the only machine to ride. It makes a statement. There is nothing that comes close to what this bike represents.

IRMA: I love riding, although I've only been a passenger. There's just something about the road and the speed and the wind—it's almost like you're flying. It's just that wonderful feeling of total freedom.

BOB GAGNON

31. California. Carpenter. Riding 12 years. 1989 FXST.

When I ride, I watch out for crazy people on the road. I keep my bike as loud as I can so they can hear me. I'm extremely careful; I've been riding twelve years and I've never dropped one yet—and I don't ever plan to. I white-line it to work everyday and I've never had any problems. I'm still okay because I'm 100 percent tuned in to what I'm doing.

I ride to get away from the everyday grind and for the freedom of the road, for the solitude and the peace it gives me.

The best reason to own a Harley is it's American made and I'm an American, and this is the only bike I can see myself on. Plus, I love the fact you can customize them and make your own individual statement.

GARY RUSKIN

45. Pennsylvania. Ex-Naval UDT; fifth-degree black belt; celebrity bodyguard. Riding 2 years. 1988 FXRSSP.

The bottom line is you have to watch out for the other guy because you're really out there all alone, and no one is going to be responsible for your safety on a motorcycle. You have to take responsibility for anticipating and reacting in a positive way to those situations that come up. I took the Motorcycle Safety Course, and it's something that can only make you more aware of how to properly handle a motorcycle. There is no room for being macho on a motorcycle.

My riding career really started because I was a personal bodyguard to a very well-known celebrity who had several Harley-Davidsons, and it really sparked an interest in me to own my own. I've put 30,000 miles on my bike in the last twenty-four months, and I would have to say I'm totally hooked on riding. It's really the nicest thing that's ever happened to me.

Why Harley? Well, it's a good bike and a great ride, and it's never let me down, but maybe the biggest thing is it's made in the U.S.A., and that is very important to me personally.

BOB CHAPMAN

43. Ohio. Tax and real estate consultant. Riding 20 years. 1988 Heritage.

I keep my head on straight when I ride. It's a spiritual thing. You've got to be one with the bike, and you have to understand your immediate surroundings. It's sort of like the same rules you have in life—you've got to respect the vehicles around you and give everybody that extra margin and keep yourself healthy. Never ride over your head, and definitely no hotdogging. I've got twenty years on a bike and I've never been down. Just stay one step ahead of them.

Riding takes away the tension of everyday living in a hectic business world. It's a good feeling, and I enjoy the wind and the road. I couldn't ever imagine not riding.

Harley is a feel, an attitude. I'm not the same person without my Harley. It's an ingredient and a component into a personality that changes the whole atmosphere of how you feel and how you look at things.

KENNY LUMBINO

37. New Jersey. Stockbroker. Riding 7 years. 1987 FLXR Low Rider Custom.

My No. 1 thing is not to ride in the morning or evening rush hours. Those people only have getting to where they're going on their minds, and the streets are totally out of control in those time frames. I went to the Advanced Motorcycle Training Course and learned to do things on this bike that I thought I'd never do, and I recommend that course to everyone. You will come out of there so much better for the experience. I'll tell you another thing that really helped. Give everyone the right-of-way who wants it. You cannot win against a 5,000-pound car.

Nothing does for me what my motorcycle does. I'm an expert skydiver, and that is about the only thing that comes close to this sensation. You become one with the world. I feel closer to God when I'm on my bike. It's a spiritual thing for sure.

Nothing looks or sounds or feels or rides like a Harley-Davidson motorcycle. No other motorcycle I've ever ridden makes me feel this alive inside. When I'm on a canyon road and I hear the thunder coming out of the pipes, I know why I'm riding a Harley.

BILLY WESTBROOK

34. California. Master custom bike builder. Riding 18 years. 1989 FXST.

Riding to me is all instinct. I don't think about anything but enjoying the moment. Basically I become part of my machine when I'm on it, and I'm fully aware that it's us against them, so I'm not unconscious out there. Of course after eighteen years of riding, your abilities are second nature to you.

You know, I stopped riding for a few years because it used to be with the old choppers we rode you couldn't go a mile without being hassled about your taillights, or your front end being too long, or your pipes being too loud. In the last few years, that's all changed, and there is a totally different atti-

tude toward motorcyclists. There is a whole world of professional people involved in motorcycling. My clients are lawyers and engineers and movie stars and I guess, in part, these people have brought a lot of credibility to the sport. I started out telling you why I ride, and I guess my answer is going to be repetitive, but it's for the freedom. I really feel motorcycling runs through my blood.

You want to know why I'm on a Harley-Davidson? You ride on a Harley and you feel like a king, that's why I'm on this motorcycle.

JOE STELLA

34. Illinois. Road dog, music business (manager). Riding 19 years. 1989 Springer.

I start out by saying a little prayer. Seriously though, you've got to relax and be confident with your machine and yourself. The little things you focus on will help keep you safe, for example when you come to a red light and you're behind an auto, leave yourself room to use the white line to go around him if someone is approaching from the rear at an unsafe speed. Stay in your mirrors, even if you're sitting dead still. That guy coming up behind you might be taking a nap and use you to help stop his car.

I ride for therapy. You go out on the road with some of these rock groups and you're ready to climb the walls after two weeks of touring. I get on my machine and it all goes away. We don't need psychiatrists, just Harleys.

My first bike was an Indian motorcycle, and I've been a V-twin lover ever since. It used to be that you had to work on your Harleys to keep them going. Now you don't have to touch them, except for a service. They just run and run. Another thing, I'm only 135 pounds, and you get on a little plastic bike and you're out there on that freeway and a truck comes by—you're ready to go kite flying. You get on 650 pounds of steel and the story is different.

KEITH BALL

42. California. Editor, Easyriders magazine and four other Paisano Publications. Riding 26 years.
1988 Evolution in a rigid frame/kickstart.

I always ride aggressively when I'm on the open highway. I ride like a sailor sails his ship across the ocean. It's a graceful thing, and I ride for the oneness of me and my motorcycle. When I ride in traffic, I ride as if I were a warrior, and all these people in their cars are out to get me. If you ride with this attitude, all your senses are electrified, and you're totally tuned in to what you're doing. Probably between the hours of 11 p.m. and 3 a.m. in the morning, you have to be that much more conscious of what's going on around you. People are leaving taverns and restaurants, and they've been drinking—it can be particularly dangerous between those hours.

I've always been very creative, and I find that riding a motorcycle and being part of it goes along with that theme of creativity. I built my own bike, and in a way I am an artist of sorts, the only difference being that unlike a painting on the wall, I can straddle my motorcycle and ride my creation across the highways.

Harley-Davidson has always epitomized the concept of taking a beautiful machine and expressing your own personality by customizing it to your taste. It's endless what you can do with one of these machines. The biker lifestyle and Harley-Davidson run through my blood. They're part of who I am.

STEVE GERBER

51. New Jersey. Investment banker. Riding 25 years. 1984 FXST.

Throughout the years I've always ridden looking for the worst-case scenario. If I'm approaching a stop sign, I just assume the other guy is going to run it; if that person's there getting ready to make a left turn, I'm always thinking that just when I get a few yards away from him, he's going to pull out. If you ride anticipating that everyone will be doing exactly what you don't want them to do, you'll be riding for a long time. I have twenty-five years on motorcycles and I haven't dumped one yet. I have to believe I owe it totally to my attitude.

I guess, for me, my bike is the closest thing to a magic carpet.

You really don't explain Harley-Davidson to anybody. Even if they don't ride, they know.

BENITO "BENI" FABRE

48. New York. Semi-retired. Riding 36 years. 1989 Softail.

I ride totally defensively all the time. You must drive for everyone else if you expect to survive on a motorcycle. I absolutely never daydream. This sport requires you to stay right there mentally; you can create problems for yourself by giving it only some of your attention. I never play with speed. I respect it, and I respect my bike. It can do a lot of things well, as long as you do not abuse it. Your bike performs only as well as you can operate it.

This is my therapy. I don't need psychiatrists. Someone else can go sit on a couch for an hour; I have this. My friends and I relive the '50s every time we get together with our bikes. It's really like being in the old neighborhood again. You know you're on your own when you're riding. It's you, the bike and God . . . really nothing else.

I ride a Harley-Davidson because I can't fly like a bird— but at least I'm close.

REED SMITH

37. California. Actor/Producer/Cowboy. Riding 25 years. 1988 Heritage.

When I was younger, I would ride without a lot of regard for myself when it came to being safe. Now I am so cautious, I break for green lights. Life is valuable, and it can really be enhanced on a motorcycle if you're responsible about it.

I remember back in 1967, I was riding my first Harley and when I went out on a date I'd have to hide the bike from the girl's parents, otherwise they'd never let her see me again. Today, the first thing a girl asks you when you ask her out is, "Do you own a Harley?". Times have changed.

I just like cruising and coming home safely. I guess part of me is still a little kid inside because when I get on my bike I go back to the feelings I had as a young boy—part cowboy and part James Dean. I've been around horses all my life, and the only difference is that this horse is made of steel.

Harley-Davidson is a motorcycle. Everything else is a sewing machine.

JIM CRAIG

35. Michigan. Contractor/Musician. Riding 26 years. 1960 Panhead.

I don't fantasize when I ride my bike. It's almost like a Zen experience. I'm totally into the moment, staying aware of everything. It's funny, when I drive my car my mind is always racing in different directions, but on my motorcycle I'm 100 percent there. It's really this type of concentration you need to survive the sport. When I'm in traffic, the only thing to assume is that all the cars are going to do exactly what you don't want them to do, and that philosophy will keep you prepared for the unexpected.

I ride for the freedom of it all. It's the old cliché, I do it just to be in the wind.

What do I think about Harleys? Well, I'm building another one similar to the one in this photo, and this bike I'm on is thirty years old and probably worth four times what you could have bought it for in 1960. That's really what Harleys are all about: an incredible value for the money.

ARTHUR "CORKY" RICE

41. Ohio. Co-owner of fifteen Budget Rent-a-Car dealerships, specializing in rental of exotic automobiles. Riding for 17 years. 1990 FXST.

Don't do anything crazy and don't take chances. I don't split lanes and I ride with a little bit of fear. I also try to avoid riding in the rain or late at night. You're not visible enough, and debris on the road is difficult to see. Sometimes when you're riding, you start to feel invincible, and I fight that perception. With me, cars always have the right-of-way because they're bigger.

I enjoy the freedom of the open air; you see life differently on a motorcycle. It's reminiscent of cowboys and Indians—it reminds me of the Old West. I like the fact that there are no social boundaries. Some riders are famous and some are not; the bike makes you all the same. I enjoy riding with a bunch of guys, just experiencing the brotherhood of it all.

Why Harley? Well, I stopped riding for a while, and when I got back into it, I went out and bought a different brand of bike. I kept it for exactly two days, and you know the rest of that story.

BEN WEISS

37. California. Assistant TV director. Riding 10 years. 1990 Sportster.

I try not to ride in the city that much. I feel your chances for error go up if you're constantly in heavy traffic. I like to get away from everything to really ride with peace of mind. Of course, you have to ride with respect for the machine and not get crazy on it. I don't consciously think about what I do to stay safe, but I guess it's fair to say that my attitude is to ride responsibly.

Riding is the only thing I've found that sort of frees my soul. You see life much more clearly from the seat of one of these machines. Riding my bike is an adventure.

I've always liked the way Harleys look, even when I didn't have one. You know, it's a little Walter Mitty-type thing; you have your straight job, and you get off work and you get on that bike and it's another world. I'll tell you something that's special for me—I am still out cruising with the guys that I first started riding with. The brotherhood and friendships are lasting.

JOAN OLSON

32. California. Group benefits specialist. Riding 2 years. 1988 Sportster.

There are some things I don't do: I never pass on the right for obvious reasons, nor do I ride alone on the freeway at night; you're not visible enough. I've taken the motorcycle safety course, and it's a big part of my consciousness toward safe riding. I've had some very good friends who taught me about surviving the traffic and the madness of Los Angeles freeways. You minimize the risks by assuming that everyone is going to pull out in front of you or do what you don't want them to do. You don't drop your guard when you are riding. Also, being a woman on a Harley, you get a lot of people who will literally change lanes to take a look at you, and that little piece of foolishness can be a danger. Sometimes they get too close for comfort.

It's exciting to ride—I love it, and also the skill to control the machine is part of the whole experience. It's just right.

When I decided to buy a bike, I looked at a lot of different motorcycles, but I kept coming back to Harley. And then a friend had this one for sale and I knew it was destined to be mine. Harley is a riding experience that cannot be put into words.

BOOMER BILLINGSLEA

60. California. Artist. Riding 43 years. 1988 FXST.

I was taught on an old Indian motorcycle by a man who was very wise about riding motorcycles—my uncle. He instilled in me that you have to respect an engine, and it will take care of you. Also, I never try to break any records on the highway, and I never try to outrun automobiles. They can have the right-of-way. When I approach someone on the verge of making a left turn, I watch him until I'm completely past him, because he'll fool you every time. Just when you think it's safe, he'll dart out in front of you, and we all know the

end of that story. I raced for twenty-five years—flat track and motocross, so I have a tremendous respect for the power and capabilities of the motorcycle, and also for the limitations of my own skills.

Why do I ride? It's really in my blood, it's part of who I am, and I just love it.

Forty-three years of riding motorcycles and today there are nine Harleys sitting in my garage. All I can tell you is when they take me away, I hope I'm sitting on one of them.

TOM ROACH

46. Wyoming. Retail executive. Riding 30 years. 1990 Fat Boy.

I don't ride worrying about getting hurt. I started out at fifteen years of age riding broncos, and almost immediately went to racing motorcycles and automobiles. I've always done things that people consider dangerous, but I never focus on that. I just try to stay aware and be defensive. I use the same attitude on the street that I did on the racetrack. Maybe the best advice is always leave yourself an out, so when you get in that tight spot, you've got a way to go.

I like the feeling of riding. I use motorcycling to get rid of my stress. I just recently rode with my eighteen-year-old son, side by side from Colorado to California, and we're now planning another trip together.

About Harleys, well they're not that far removed from the Old West. I often think about my past involvement with horses and bronc riding, and as far as I'm concerned, I'm still on a horse.

MITCH LIEBER

37. Securities broker. Massachusetts. Riding 21 years. 1989 Heritage.

Occasionally I ride my motorcycle to work, and on those particular days I take everything I know about safety and multiply it. There's no getting around it, in the morning rush hours people are basically oblivious to you. Really, the thing you have to do is adjust your riding to the circumstances. If you're out there in the country, you're obviously not going to be as intense as if you were on a freeway at 7:30 in the morning. I really slowed up a lot with this bike. It's definitely a cruiser, and all the nonsense about racing around is just not what this machine is all about. I've become very conservative with this motorcycle.

I ride for the freedom. Sometimes it might be a spiritual thing and, if it's not, it usually becomes so. Somehow my time with my motorcycle becomes my private retreat.

Harley-Davidson is American and it's what I grew up looking at as my idea of a motorcycle. It might be the Marlon Brando thing, I don't know. It feels so good; that image, the look, the machine—it's all there.

BILL KLING

45. California. Certified public accountant; co-founder of the Cheesecake Factory. Riding 34 years.
Personal bikes, 2 Harley-Davidsons and 7 Indian motorcycles.

My rules for taking care of myself are: I don't feel comfortable with splitting traffic, even though it's allowed, so I have a tendency to find my comfort level and to drive in it; I always assume the driver of any car can't see me, so my lights are on all the time, and I make my presence known. I never crowd an automobile, and I never hot-rod my machine. The key is to ride well within your abilities.

I ride for the same reasons I fly a plane. The sensations are very similar. You're free. After a while, I don't even feel like there's a bike under me. I feel like I'm out there flying.

As a child I can remember seeing Harleys and Indians on the road. Times were different then, and those bikes were almost a no-no because they were given a bad image through the media. But the lure of the bikes, especially the Indians, and the fact that they weren't being made anymore was a combination that fascinated me and drew me to motorcycling. For me, it was the name, the look, the headdress, the emblem on the tank ... virtually everything got me to fall in love, first with Indian motorcycles and then with Harleys. As far as Harleys are concerned, the new Harleys are fabulous machines and, for my money, the finest motorcycle ever made. I've been into airplanes, street rods, boating, but the people in this sport don't care what you have or who you are—the machine and the wind are the bond.

ED ROWLETT

34. California. Custom motorcycle painter. Riding 18 years. 1982 Harley Super Glide with 1971 body parts.

After all these years I guess it's fair to say it's all second nature to me, as far as being safe when I ride my bike. But it's really as simple as being focused on what's going on around you. Potential problems can really be avoided by anticipation and being tuned in. Listen, I'm riding eighteen years and I haven't hit the street once. I'm sure a part of it is luck, but I work at staying healthy, and paying attention is really the key.

I'm riding because it's the only thing that clears my head and leaves me in a good way. I'm on this bike every single day, and it's a medicine of sorts.

Nothing made anywhere comes close to what Harley-Davidson has captured. It's pride, steel and power.

DAVID MANN • JACKIE MANN

David: 49. Missouri. Commercial artist/Illustrator of motorcycle lore. Riding 30 years.
1957 Panhead with a shovelhead top end/jockey shift.
Jackie: 41. New York. Assistant to the artist.

DAVID: Ride carefully, and always be conscious of being defensive. When I have someone on the back of my bike, I am that much more responsible. I've learned from some of the tight spots I've been in, and hopefully you commit those to memory and try not to let them happen again. I spend more time looking out for the other guy than any other thing I do to stay safe. Also, you have to vary your speed according to the conditions. Sometimes the posted speed limit might be too fast because of the circumstances. It's just common sense.

I ride because it frees me from all the pressures that I have in my life. I'm fortunate in that I make a large part of my living depicting the biker life-style through my art, and here my personal passion is also motorcycles. I would like to mention

that a lot of people don't realize that I illustrate book covers for publishers, and I've done over 350 covers on subjects not related to motorcycles.

I ride Harley-Davidson motorcycles because they're American, and it's been my experience that everyone who doesn't have one wishes he did. They sound good, they look good, and I'm so thankful that they're part of my life.

JACKIE: I have never experienced anything as exciting as being on a Harley-Davidson in the wind. It's really a rush, and I think the feeling of total freedom that it gives you is the reward.

ZACHARY HOLLAND

51. New York. Actor/Director. Riding 6 years. 1989 FLHDC.

I do exactly what I was taught in motorcycle training school when I ride: scan, interpret, predict, and execute. I'm always scanning my mirrors for autos approaching from behind. I never do stupid things. This sport is total common sense; don't push. I ride a bike 365 days a year, and often it's raining or there's very heavy traffic. But just by applying yourself 100 percent, you can ride successfully.

Every time I get on this bike, it's an adventure. I ride because it's a matter of preference, it's an event for me.

There's no such thing as a traffic jam for me—thirty miles an hour is my idea of a traffic jam.

I was always in awe of Harley-Davidsons. I love the mystique and the pride. I've been to Milwaukee and had a tour of the plant. As far as I'm concerned, Harley stands for every bit of integrity that's American and for the American myth.

MARK MELTZER

28. California. Hairdresser. Riding 9 years. 1982 FLH.

You don't need me to tell you it's crazy on the streets. So when you get on your machine, you'd better plug your brain into what's going on around you. This sport can be so enjoyable and anxiety free, if you treat it with the respect it requires. I guess to sum it up in a couple of words, just stay alert.

This is my toy, and riding this bike lets me really unwind and rejuvenate my energies. It is without a doubt the most enjoyable pastime that you can have as an adult. There are so many incredible moments associated with riding.

There really isn't another brand of bike I would consider owning. I almost feel that if Harley-Davidson weren't around, I wouldn't be riding. This machine is a large part of the magic of motorcycling.

LYCIA NAFF

26. Nevada. Actress/Poet. Riding 2 years. 1988 Sportster.

I ride defensively, but mainly I make sure that other people are aware that I am there. I have loud pipes on my bike, and I believe this is a big help in being visible. I wouldn't say I'm "Miss Safety," but I am very careful, well trained, and alert. If I do happen to take a risk, it's calculated. A movie I was involved in required that I ride a motorcycle so I went to motorcycle training school. The second day there I bought this bike you see now. I knew instantly that I was meant to ride a Harley, and I ride it like I'm a part of it.

I guess I would like to go on record saying I was born to ride. At least, that's how it feels to me. You can't get me off this bike, and it is part of who I am.

I would only ride or, better yet, own a Harley or an Indian motorcycle. I love that it's American, and the way that it rides and feels is incredible. It's that rich, deep, sexy sound that is uniquely Harley. I would never be on anything else, and I mean never!

ERIC CHAMBERS

30. California. Stuntman/Pilot. Riding 20 years. 1983 FLH.

Being a stuntman, the word "safety" is ingrained in me, and that attitude carries over to my motorcycle riding and also to flying an airplane. I don't hotdog and I keep my distance from cars, because the way the story always goes is, "I didn't see you." I never hit that maximum speed where I could lose control of the situation. I get enough thrills at work. I just cruise and take it easy. There's no margin for error, whether you're flying an airplane or doing stunts and, for sure, there's none on a motorcycle.

I ride for the peacefulness it gives me. I feel a little like a locomotive chugging down the road; the rhythm of the motor is soothing. Also, I enjoy the social part of Harley-Davidson.

This is absolutely, as far as I'm concerned, the only machine. It's quality and steel and pride of ownership.

MAX HUSHAHN

28. West Germany. Writer/Director. Riding 10 years. 1989 Heritage, 1988 FXST.

I have no fear of the bike; I'm not worried about getting hurt. I mean, I'm safe and alert, but if something were to happen I could deal with it. Maybe it's that Jimmy Dean feeling— there's an edge to riding. You're so alive, but so close to danger. Don't misunderstand this, because I plan on living a long life. But as a writer, there is a romantic part of how I perceive motorcycling. I've done a lot of dirt biking, and my skills on a motorcycle are something I have a lot of confidence in. I

don't freeze up in situations that could be trouble. The knowledge I have gives me power to think and ride my way through the danger.

It's a cliché. It's the feeling of freedom, nothing around you, just the wind. You feel like a cowboy on a steel horse.

Harley, well it's the styling and the sound and the image. It goes back to *Easy Rider* and *The Wild One.*

JOHN BARON • DEBRA BARON

John: 47. China. Automobile business. Riding 25 years. 1988 FXST.
Debra: 39. Massachussetts. School teacher.

JOHN: I try to stay alert to the extreme; my senses are tuned in. You have to be anticipating everything at all times; you can't just cruise around unconsciously. Automobile drivers are not going to be doing your job for you. You've got to be responsible for your safety on a bike. I guess there's an element of luck, because there are things you can't control. But if you're not paying attention, all the luck in the world won't help you.

I ride because it's cheaper than therapy. It gives me an outlet for my frustrations, and this is a healthy release for me. I can simply say that I enjoy riding tremendously.

I left China when I was ten years old, and we wound up in a kind of ghetto in Los Angeles. There were guys in the neighborhood on Harleys back then, and I guess you can say that's where my interest was developed. I'm 100 percent pro Harley-Davidson. It's the only motorcycle.

DEBRA: I love the way you can experience the air currents and sit back and watch the country roll on by, plus I get to spend some great moments with my husband. I act as the navigator, planning out the route on maps. This is a wonderful part of our relationship.

THE IRON STALLION

HARLEY-DAVIDSON

CELEBRITY INTERVIEW

COURTNEY CALDWELL

40. California. Publisher, American Woman Road Riding magazine; founder/president American Women Road Riders Alliance; cable TV producer/hostess, American Rider; participant in Van Buren Transcon; mother. Riding 10 years. 1989 FXRS.

Riding my Harley up into the mountains, along the coast, or through scenic backroads...getting out of the city and away from traffic affords me the greatest riding pleasure in safe yet challenging conditions. On one exciting trip soloing from Wisconsin to Los Angeles, it was my new Low Rider, the elements and me!

I ride motorcycles because of the effect it has on my spirit. It's a natural high. Riding and tae kwon do are the only things I've experienced that unite my mind, body, heart, and soul. There's a connection I can only describe as spiritual, which seems to reach deep into my essence like nothing else. I can't imagine my life without them.

My multiple careers keep me busy, and balancing them all with time for my family tends to keep stress levels working overtime. Riding eliminates that stress completely and keeps me sane.

I started riding ten years ago on smaller bikes. I thought owning a Harley would always be just a dream. After all, when you're 5'1", female, and from RI, things like that don't happen in real life. The desire to own a Harley goes far beyond anything that can be explained—it's something you feel, you know, you belong with. Harley-Davidson knew exactly what they were talking about when they said, "Things are different on a Harley."

VIC KING

46. Massachusetts. Owner of Vic's Custom Cycles. Riding 25 years. 1938 Knucklehead.

Riding is really simple—ride defensively and you will be riding safe. Never underestimate the bike or it will bite you hard. Respect your equipment, and remember all that power will be your friend if you don't abuse it. Most of the problems I've seen when it comes to motorcycling have been from a blatant disregard for safety.

Riding for me is not only a livelihood, it's a way of life. It's in my blood. For twenty-five years now, it's been a big part of who I am. The friendships and good times I've shared because of motorcycling are really the highlights of my life.

What about Harley-Davidson? Well, I'll tell you this, when I'm gone and you're gone, Harley will still be here.

JOE ALTADONNA

60. Michigan. Production designer of movie sets. Riding 20 years. 1978 FLH.

I ride totally on the defensive, and when I ride with my friends we all give each other plenty of room for anything unexpected. You know you're not sitting on a very big item, so it takes complete concentration to stay there. Common sense, concentration and knowledge about the limitations of a motorcycle will go a long way.

Motorcycle riding is actually the cheapest entertainment I know. For $3 in gas I can ride around all day and feel like I've been on a vacation. I don't know anyone who has tried this sport and not fallen in love with it. Even the people who do not ride are fascinated with riding a Harley-Davidson.

This bike is one of two Harleys I own, and they are my passion and an endless source of pleasure.

LARRY GRODSKY

39. Pennsylvania. Motorcycling Safety Instructor. Photographed with a Harley-Davidson Buell.

EXPERIENCE SPEAKS—A Special Interview on Motorcycling Safety

CARMEN: How long have you been riding a motorcycle?

LARRY: I started riding twenty years ago this month in Athens, Ohio, the site of the big AMA bash this summer honoring the opening of the new American Heritage Motorcycle Museum.

CARMEN: How long have you been teaching people how to instruct other people on how to ride motorcycles?

LARRY: That would be ten years this month. I've spent half of my riding career teaching others to ride. I got involved through a friend at a local community college, and I'm still teaching with the same organization. I have about 200 students a year. Most of them are novice riders, although certainly not all of them. Occasionally I do an Experienced Rider Course as well, as I do seminars through *Rider* magazine.

CARMEN: On the Experienced Rider Course?

LARRY: Well, not necessarily. When I say the Experienced Rider Course, that's in quotes. That's a Motorcycle Safety Foundation program. I also do seminars of my own design.

CARMEN: Tell me about teaching people when it comes to the advanced motorcycle riding course. What does that entail?

LARRY: That's a one-day event. Essentially what we work on is certainly attitude, but for somebody at that level, we usually recommend that people take that course. They should have a minimum of one year experience and say 5,000 miles under their belt, although that's somewhat flexible. We work on what I call the big three: strong braking, steering, and flexibility, which I'm sure we will get more into later. The third is the ability to predict hazards in traffic. I think any safety program has got to focus on those three things—they are most identified as being absent among accidents involving cyclists.

CARMEN: I'm sure there are all kinds of variables that we could talk about when it comes to riding a motorcycle successfully.

LARRY: If I could just jump in here a second. One thing that we try to do is instill a system of thought in a rider so that he or she can address each new situation to react quickly and intuitively, and correctly I would hope.

CARMEN: So in this course you take the experienced rider or someone with a few hundred miles under his belt, and I'm assuming that you must start him out with the dynamics of braking, right?

LARRY: We start them with about three-and-a-half hours of classroom work where we cover everything. The very first thing we do on the motorcycles is a kind of warm-up drill in which we evaluate their skills just to make sure that they truly belong in an experienced rider course. The next thing is the principles of stopping.

CARMEN: With all those miles of experience and all those students, obviously a few thousand people have benefited from your knowledge. Tell us about braking.

LARRY: I think braking is the single most absent skill among the average rider, and I have my own theory. Most people in our country learn to drive an automobile before they learn to ride a motorcycle. Even though you have a foot pedal in a similar location, and they are both operated with the right foot, the actual skill is so much different because a motorcycle has two brakes. Since the weight shifts forward during deceleration the lion's share of the stopping force goes to the front of the brake. What we find to be the most common error in braking is that people instinctively mash down on the foot brake as they would in a car, locking up their rear brake. Another typical error is when a person locks up his rear brake, then panics and suddenly releases the rear brake after he's locked it up. This can cause a high side. In other words, it can cause the bike to swap ends. The rear wheel, when it starts to make power again, would drive around in front of the front wheel. Everyone occasionally locks up his back brake, and it's not such a big deal. There is a way to release it gradually so that you don't cause a high side. The main thing is good steady pressure on the front brake, and I think the only way to achieve that is by repetition. A teenager can probably grasp the fundamentals of balancing, shifting, and stopping a motor in a few minutes if there is an emergency situation, and I think the average person's natural reaction again is to mash down on the foot brake, which is quite opposite from what you want to do to bring the bike to a smooth, secure stop. I never use the term "panic stop." I don't think it has any place in our vocabulary. I emphasize control, so call it an emergency stop if you will. Control and smoothness are the things I always strive for.

CARMEN: I can totally relate to the swapping ends, because it has happened to me. I am older; I'm not a teenager and maybe that was it. I overreacted and locked up the rear. On both occasions I never even touched the front brake. They were instant situations that popped right in front of me and my foot just went down. Both of these happened quite a while ago, and hopefully it will never happen again. I make it a practice now that at every light I stop at, whether it be a stoplight, stop sign, whatever reason there is that I need to stop my bike, I use my front brake so that hopefully the next time this happens (which I'm sure it will) I'm going to go for that front brake. In fact, this friend of mine took a Desmond tour in Europe, and he disconnected his rear brake for the entire tour, which I think was through the Italian Alps.

LARRY: I know that tour, and one of the things they tell you is to never use your rear brake.

CARMEN: Tell me about that. When you're in turns that are severe and some of them are basically switchbacks, I guess, with a lot of decreasing-radius turns and you don't have a rear brake—would you explain that?

LARRY: There is a school of thought, mostly among racers, that the rear brake is of no value. All that rear brake does is get you in trouble. I don't necessarily subscribe to that school of thought, although I fully understand where they're coming from. In racing the deceleration is so rapid, the transfer of weight onto the front brake or wheel is so rapid it renders your rear brake almost useless. The effect of your rear brake is just a product of how rapidly your front brake is applied. I should also consider the weight of your bike, the proportion of front to rear weight; for instance, a lightweight sport bike has less need of a rear brake probably than that of a great big touring bike because the big bike is going to keep some weight on the rear wheel. To get to the situation in the Alps: You may not have the racetrack speeds, but you have the fact of the steepness entering into the picture. If you can picture in your mind a motorcycle tilted on its front wheel; that's the situation that you have when you're braking, when you're going downhill in those very steep Alps. Once again it takes very little pressure on the back brake to lock it up.

CARMEN: There is no weight being carried back there?

LARRY: Correct.

CARMEN: So when you're in a straight line and not in the Alps and you use your brakes correctly, you're actually compressing the entire suspension evenly by using the back and front at the same time. In the situation you're talking about, you can't get that balance because you don't have the weight; it transfers all wrong. Is that it?

LARRY: That's pretty much it. I would not say that the suspension is compressing evenly, because you're going to always have much more compression on the front, but in principle you're right. As I said, I'm not ready to endorse front-wheel-only braking, but I certainly recognize where those people are coming from. It may come down to that. In the future you may be seeing bikes being built with very, very tiny rear brakes. I just don't know. I don't have a crystal ball. I think anybody could see how much trouble they could get themselves into by overbraking on the rear and overbraking on the front.

CARMEN: If you're in a turn, you're using your front brakes sparingly because you can wash that wheel out, or am I misreading this?

LARRY: No, you're not misreading it at all. There's an equation that goes into effect to determine how much traction you have. Your traction is divided into various parts, traction for braking and traction for leaning. In the case of the rear wheel you have traction for driving the rear wheel. Any time you're using up part of the traction in one of these areas you have that much less to devote to another one. If you lean over full tilt, scraping your knee on the pavement, you clearly can't squeeze full pressure on your brake; as you said, you will wash out both of your wheels. You break traction completely, but when you lean over more moderately with the proper leaning angles you still have a sizable portion of breaking traction left to administer. Which is why you always want to leave something in reserve. That's the difference between riding on the street and riding on a racetrack. Riding on the street you always have to leave something in reserve.

CARMEN: As opposed to a racetrack where it's controlled and there are no curbs, sidewalks, or automobiles pulling out in front of you. Is there something you can say or give us to put us in a mindset to be successful in front-braking down on your motorcycle in an emergency situation? Is there something you can focus on and mull over and work with, like a mental exercise to help with that?

LARRY: I recommend physical exercise. I would say the most important thing is to practice. There's something I do sometimes in my seminars, just to get people the feel of controlling the bike with their fingers. I personally don't care whether you use two or four fingers, it makes no difference. The important thing is that you can stop the bike in the shortest possible distance. A little drill is to have people start out with both feet on the pegs going only fast enough to balance the motorcycle without wobbling. If the bike wobbles, you're going too slowly. We're talking five mph. The drill is to keep your eyes pointed well down the road and just squeeze the front brake where your forks bottom out.

Naturally they will rebound, but you keep your knees glued to the gas tank while this is happening till the forks are fully rebound, and then you put your feet down. That gives you the feeling of controlling that front-end dive and controlling the deceleration of the bike with just your little fingers. It connects the bike to the fingers, which is the way it should be. You will find that you gradually pick up speed. Usually what happens when I do that drill is that people start out at five mph and before I know it they're going twenty mph and I have to tell them to slow down. I would do that and from there on in I would just practice. I think if you can consistently make really good stops at twenty-five mph, then you'll probably be fine at sixty mph. Statistically you're much more likely to execute an emergency stop at twenty-five than you are at sixty.

CARMEN: I find myself doing what you suggested without realizing it, but when I don't have a specific destination in mind, and I'm just out there, and come to a stop light, I find myself playing around, trying to get closer and closer to that light before I brake, with the knowledge that I have plenty of room to stop, but just trying to get closer to see if I could shorten the distance on my front-brake stopping techniques, which is like an exercise. I don't bring my knees into the tank as you suggested, but I'll try now. It's a good feeling when you know you can stop your bike in a matter of twenty-five or thirty feet. Especially when you're coming down from maybe thirty mph.

LARRY: That's just about what it should take, about thirty feet, at thirty mph. That's a damn good stop. Let me add one more thing. I keep emphasizing the importance of not panicking. It should always be smooth. You don't want to grab at the brake lever because you have to allow time for the weight to settle onto the front wheel (that's when skids or lockups occur), and then it breaks traction.

CARMEN: Right, I think I follow what you're saying. In other words, you're braking and the pressure's being applied consistently but gradually, as opposed to stabbing it.

LARRY: Exactly. If you would, imagine a bike stopping in slow motion: You could see a bike coming down the road with a slow-motion camera on it; you see how the forks can dip. That period while the forks are dipping, that's weight settling on the front wheel. An overly aggressive application of the front brake is going to make that front-wheel-brake traction.

CARMEN: This might not even apply, but are we saying that if your front end doesn't have a lot of play in it, for instance, and that the front springs are really firm, or you have the right

fork oil in there, you won't have all that transfer of all that weight?

LARRY: As long as we have telescopic forks, you're going to have it. That's its job. We have bikes that have anti-dive mechanisms and so forth, but under a really aggressive braking situation all that means is that the rate is going to be brought under control, but you're still going to use most of your suspension travel on a really hard stop.

CARMEN: What about riding in the wet, that takes in everything—braking and leaning, of course the road turns into glass initially. What could you tell us about riding in the rain?

LARRY: I think you just mentioned the most important thing of all when you said the streets turn into glass. I think most people are schooled in this area. Driver education teachers have done a terrific job making the public aware that the streets really do get slippery during the first fifteen minutes of a storm. That's where all that oil is raised up to the surface. It's probably much more treacherous in the Southwest than in the East, where I live. The rain is infrequent, so the oil has a much longer period to build up. Riding in the rain isn't that much different than riding in dry conditions. In fact, once the road is clear of that surface oil the amount of available traction is probably greater than most people realize. I think the problem is a physical one more than a mental one—people allow themselves to ride much more nervously instead of riding more aware or alertly. They grip the bars tighter. That really doesn't apply to riding in the rain, but if you ever notice when you get nervous your elbows start to come up. I don't know why that is, but I know it to be a fact. That's an indication to relax yourself, pull over if you have to. Try to take the tension out of your muscles. Probably the best advice is to let the motorcycle do a little more of what it wants to do. You might get a little bit of slippage here or there. You talked about gyroscope and that's what a motorcycle is. It is two big gyroscopes. You've got to give them a chance to do what they do. A lot of people automatically feel if you skid a front wheel you're going to crash, and that's not the case at all. A little skid, let it go; it will hook up again, provided you're riding in a relatively smooth manner. If you have a hand full of throttle and you mash down on the brakes, you're going to crash sooner or later anyhow. If you're a smooth rider, a little baby skid here or there is not going to spill you onto the pavement. My main advice is to slow down, relax and try to enjoy yourself, and let the bike do what it has to do. Stopping distances are going to be increased somewhat, but not that much. Allow yourself more following distance. I think perhaps the biggest danger in riding in the rain is visibility. Naturally you as a rider are most concerned with the thought of a skid or fall, but perhaps your biggest concern is whether other people see you. I think that is the biggest danger of riding in the rain. Other people just simply aren't aware. Visibility is greatly changed.

CARMEN: I know one thing, a lot of this is attitude. You started out with that word. Attitude is a sense of how you perceive what's really happening. I know you can manufacture little monsters in your mind that can cause yourself a lot of problems. I'm just relating to my own experiences of when I started riding, that didn't really exist. I remember I had a guy working for me who didn't have any transportation but a motorcycle, and it was the rainy season. Our office closed around nine p.m. Many nights it was pouring to the point that there was hardly any visibility, and he would ride home, about thirty miles, on his motorcycle. Naturally he wore full raingear. The next day I'd ask him what that was like...on the freeway, rain coming down in buckets; I knew I would have used full power on my windshield wipers in my car. He would say it was no problem, he stayed under fifty mph. It would amaze me. Here I was, thinking that the thought of being caught in a downpour would make me go sit on the side of the road, and here's a guy who'd been riding for over ten years who to that day didn't own a car and dealt with it like it was nothing. I guess it's the attitude and believing in your equipment.

LARRY: Since you mention equipment: tires. You can get by on marginal tires on a dry pavement, but it's suicidal to run on bad tires in the rain.

CARMEN: That's true, I think we all know that. To back up a little bit, what about that gyroscope effect? That bike, when you're applying power or you're just moving fractionally, just one mph—it's actually balanced. It's staying up because of the gyroscope effect. Can you tell us anything about that?

LARRY: Physics is really not my thing, but if we could move into steering I could explain to you in layman's terms what's going on when you're steering a motorcycle. I prefer to think of it as magic, instead of physics.

CARMEN: Tell us about the magic.

LARRY: If it's not magic every time you twist the throttle and feel the thing take off, balancing the way it does, then probably you should not be riding a motorcycle anymore. It presents a unique dilemma. You don't want to think about it, you just want to feel it. That's the joy of riding a motorcycle. On the other hand, your life is literally in both of your hands. I feel that you have to be of two minds. A left brain, right brain thing. Both of those brains have to be brought into balance to ride a motorcycle. First to backtrack, a motorcycle

steers the opposite of an automobile. That's what we call countersteering. Many motorcyclists know this.

CARMEN: Could you explain this further?

LARRY: By steering the motorcycle to the right, you're leaning the motorcycle to the left. I think most motorcyclists are aware of this to some level. We find that in accident situations the rider reverts to car steering. There's a whole body of accident data that suggests that people steer right into the thing that they're trying to avoid. They panic and revert back to car steering. When I first started teaching motorcycle safety, we were told to teach others that countersteering comes into effect at speeds above ten or twelve mph. That's not true; countersteering works at all speeds. Even at one mph. People are going to argue this point. You can see for yourself. You can balance a motorcycle even if it's standing still. If you can balance a motorcycle perfectly and turn the handlebars to the right, the motorcycle is going to flop over to the left. There is a certain illusion that countersteering isn't the only steering force that goes into making a turn. There's a torque steer. This is what the motorcycle does all by itself to keep from falling. You can just walk a motorcycle through a corner. If you just let the clutch out and push gently on the left handlebar, you will see the bike will lean to the left. When I say push on the left handlebar, you're actually making the handlebars turn to the right—countersteering. Your motorcycle is leaning to the left while the handlebars are turned to the right, but suddenly all by themselves the handlebars will turn back to the left and the front wheel will turn back to the left. That's torque steer. That's the motorcycle doing that all by itself, just to keep from falling. It's blocking its fall. People see that torque steer and they think that's what you're doing, that's making you negotiate the turn, when that's not true at all; that's what's keeping the bike from falling down. If you would suddenly take your hands off the handlebars it would still do that. That's why people have difficulty with low-speed turns, because they fight with the motorcycle. The motorcycle actually knows what it has to do to get through the turn. So all it takes is a gentle nudge in the way of a countersteer. All this sounds terribly complex and counter-intuitive, but what we do is we narrow it down to one simple rule, and that is: Push left, go left; push right, go right.

CARMEN: The countersteering thing.

LARRY: Right. You don't need a physics degree to remember that. After that, it's just a matter of relaxing and enjoying the ride. Of course some handlebar pressure is going to be required to maintain turns, but the thing we try to get across is that motorcycles have a sense about them. Motorcycles have a way of going through the turns if you let them and don't try to give them too many signals.

CARMEN: Talking about the turns, I know you wrote a wonderful article several months ago on slow turning. Turning these large bikes in a small area, especially the Harleys which get up to 600 or 700 pounds depending on the equipment, could seem like a great task, for instance on a two-lane road. Tell us about making slow-speed turns.

LARRY: What I've done is break this down to a six-step process, with emphasis on two things: visual direction control and relaxation. There are special techniques I'll throw in as well. If you can visualize this, you can slow down and ride the rear brake if you want, then you could squeeze the clutch in and push in the direction of the turn. All this requires is a gentle nudge in the direction of the turn. With the clutch in, the bike will literally fall. While you're doing this, you're going to turn your head in the direction of the turn. Step five is to unweight the handlebars. Really, I'm running through this step by step, but it's almost done simultaneously. You unweight the handlebars and the front end will tuck in; that's the torque steer that we talked about earlier. Since the motorcycle is falling you have to stop that fall, so you use the throttle and clutch to restabilize the bike. Of course, if you use a lot of throttle it will stabilize quite quickly and go wide; it will no longer be a tight turn, so it has to be a smooth administration of the throttle and clutch—just enough to keep your balance. One thing I mostly emphasize here is turning your head. If you look at the boundaries for the curb, you're going to hit the curb. You're going to go where you're looking, so you have to literally look over your shoulder. That would be where I would place the heaviest emphasis: Turning your head, unweighting the handlebars, and letting the motorcycle do what it has to do. Another technique that helps a lot of people with bigger bikes is to apply opposite body lean. You have probably seen pictures of road racers hanging off their motorcycles—you're doing exactly the opposite of that. That shift in the center of gravity lessens the affect of lean angle even though the motorcycle is still at a considerable lean angle. Because of the weight being on the other side, the effect of the lean angle is less. What you're actually enabling the bike to do is go slowly while it's leaned over. When you see a road racer leaning off, he is enabling the bike to go faster at the same lean angle, because he's running out of clearance. You're doing the opposite; you're enabling the bike to go slower while it's leaned over.

CARMEN: By literally placing your body in the opposite side of the turn off your seat, you're balancing out that bike and, in a sense, stabilizing it.

LARRY: Yes. Counterbalancing. Don't confuse that with countersteering. They are two entirely different principles.

CARMEN: We've covered a lot of subjects here. I found it interesting that you just said "you go where you look." I haven't heard that in a long time.

LARRY: That applies to all speeds.

CARMEN: At all speeds, you're right. You go where you look and that particularly applies going through turns, where you have to literally look through them to go where you want to go.

LARRY: A question frequently posed to students is, "At sixty mph, how many feet per second are you traveling?" I don't give them time to think about it. How many are you traveling? Carmen, don't think about it.

CARMEN: I'd say sixty feet.

LARRY: I could be generous and say you're in the ballpark.

CARMEN: Don't be generous, tell me how off the mark I am.

LARRY: It's eighty-eight feet per second. It might sound like a meaningless piece of trivia, but I don't think it is, because that's how far down the road you have to be looking—eighty-eight feet for every second.

CARMEN: I never thought about it that way.

LARRY: We tell people to maintain a twelve-second visual lead. So twelve times eighty-eight is over 1,000 feet.

CARMEN: Incredible. There's a whole lot that goes into riding one of these things successfully. What I'm trying to do with my book is make people understand how responsible you have to be. There are a lot of responsible people on motorcycles that care about safety, their own well-being, and everyone else's well-being. They don't want to just go out there and fire it up, point it, and open up the throttle. They're really concerned about getting home in one piece, because they love it. It's not a death wish, it's really a life wish to people who are riding motorcycles. It is like a celebration of life. I think sometimes when people do not ride it's hard for them to understand why someone would be sitting on a piece of metal, all exposed out there. So really, in my book and thanks to you and the people that are involved, I am trying to communicate to the non-rider that, yes, we all love riding but, guess what, we all want to stay in one piece. We all want to be responsible. I really appreciate you for your time and insight into the knowledge you've gained through twenty years of motorcycle riding, and it's been a pleasure doing this with you. Is there anything you'd like to say in closing?

LARRY: Two things: I don't put myself up as the final authority on motorcycle safety; it's just important for everyone to recognize a greater authority, even if it's only for a day. By that I mean take some of the courses. I don't care if it's an MSF course or if it's Reg Prigmore's, which he calls CLASS (California Leading Advance Safety School). I don't care what it is, but for one day put yourself at the mercy of someone that you recognize to be more expert than yourself. And another thing is, we have so many accidents at intersections. The majority of those are the automobile drivers' fault: a car turning left in front of the motorcycle. It's so avoidable. It could be avoided by positive action on the part of the motorcyclists every time they approach an intersection. Whether there's a car there with its left signal on, or whether it's just a potential for somebody to turn left in front of you, slow down, move to the right so that you can put space between yourself and the vehicle. Earlier you mentioned the roads become slippery driving during the first fifteen minutes of a rainstorm. Everybody seems to know that; it's been engraved in their minds. If everybody had that same kind of awareness of what it took to avoid getting struck by a left-turning automobile, I think we could drastically reduce the numbers of injuries and fatalities. It's just a simple matter of putting space between you and them. Don't give the driver the chance to make impact with you.

CARMEN: I interviewed Lorenzo Lamas, who has been riding motorcycles for fifteen years. During the interview I asked him what he does to keep himself in one piece. He said, "I stay away from cars. I keep a lot of distance between me and the cars." And that's what you just said.

LARRY: It's motorcycle safety in a nutshell.

CARMEN: I like to think of it as playing chess. I drive a lot in my automobile. I put on over 50,000 miles a year in California alone, because of the nature of what I was doing prior to publishing this book. I see a lot of things on the road in that car. Because I'm a motorcyclist, I see it from a motorcyclist's viewpoint. I like to play chess with the other cars in my mind, and I try to put myself in their places, try to figure out what they're going to do. I think that's how you have to ride. What are the variables here? What could happen and what am I going to do? When I ride, I'm always thinking, "Where am I going to put this thing?" Especially when I go through an intersection—I don't care if it's green. How many times have we all gone through an intersection and had that guy run the light? Or seen a guy sitting at the light and just because he thought it was his turn he goes? Somebody rang a bell, and he says, "I'm going now." I think that's the attitude you have to have. Put a lot of space between you and the car. Play chess when you're on the road, and figure out what that guy's going to do. It is definitely not a sport to be daydreaming in.

LARRY: Chess is a good analogy. I think I'm going to steal that from you.

CARMEN: Steal that from me, go ahead. Larry, you're great. I appreciate this so much, and I thank you for your time. I know it's valuable. It's great to talk to someone who's been out there for twenty years on a motor, who has the right attitude and knows how to play the game. I really feel you're an educator when it comes to this subject. I consider it a privilege to have you give me your thoughts on safety. Take care of yourself. And thank you, Larry.

MEMORIES WITH MY DAD

By Chad McQueen

He was a hero to the world, but to me he was just my dad.

I can still feel the wind in my face from that first ride when my father, Steve McQueen, put me on his lap and took me for a ride on his Triumph. All of five years old, I was hooked. A year later my dad gave me my first motorcycle—a Benillie mini cycle. I rode that thing till the wheels came off.

By the time I was nine, I was racing mini cycles. At thirteen, I won my class in the World Mini Grand Prix, but my dad was already pretty tired of taking me all over the country so I was forced into an early retirement.

Palm Springs was still a small old-fashioned town then, with lots of open space. One of my dad's favorite trips was to pack up and head out there. He'd wake me up in the morning and we'd ride dirt bikes out in the desert. That feeling of freedom is something I've never been able to get out of my blood to this day.

Around 1973 my father developed an interest in antique motorcycles. The interest soon became an obsession, and when I wasn't in school I would join him as he traveled around the country searching for old bikes. Most of the time he'd find them rotting away in some farmer's barn out in Missouri. He'd ship them back to Los Angeles and have them restored to showroom condition. Indians and Harley-Davidsons were his passions.

Once again I found myself riding with my father in a new and completely different world . . . cruising down Pacific Coast Highway on pre-World War II Harleys. Whenever we got pulled over the police officers were more interested in checking out the bikes than writing me a ticket for being underage—they never did write me up.

At the time of my father's death, November 7, 1980, his collection had grown to 127 antique motorcycles. In fact, if you pass through Las Vegas today, you can see several U.S. Army-issue pre-World War II Harley-Davidsons from my dad's collection on display at the Imperial Palace Hotel.

Today I ride everything from a 1909 belt-drive to a 1990 Springer Softail. I still love going for an early morning ride down the coast highway, feeling that wind in my face, enjoying the freedom I have grown accustomed to. Live to ride, ride to live.

THE HELMET CONTROVERSY:
Should Those who ride decide?

By Wayne Thomas

As the co-director of the California Motorcyclist Association (CMA) I am constantly asked my opinion about the effectiveness of mandatory adult helmet laws. Unfortunately there is no simple answer to the question, but there are definitely strong opinions in each camp.

There are several different groups of people with opinions on the issue. They are: 1) the non-riding public whose usual opinion is that helmets are just like seat belts and probably are a good thing, so everyone should wear one; 2) the non-riding public who believe that Americans should have a choice on issues like seat belts and helmets; 3) the rider who is pro-helmet and thinks that everyone should wear a helmet and that anyone who doesn't is crazy; 4) the rider who is anti-helmet and thinks that no one should wear a helmet and that anyone who does is crazy; and last, but certainly not least, 5) the riders who may or may not wear a helmet, but believe it should be up to the individual riders to analyze their own skills and the conditions of the day and decide the issue for themselves. It is important to note that there is a big change in opinions when one qualifies the question by separating adults (those over eighteen years of age) from those under eighteen years of age. Riders obviously feel more strongly about it than most. And it is not without good reason, as the demographics of the Harley rider are slightly different from that of the average rider.

According to the most recent consumer research, the average rider in the U.S. is a middle-class male, of which over half are married. Over half have a high school education while over a third have a college education and/or degree. Of the owners surveyed, the majority falls into three categories; twenty-two percent were semi-skilled laborers, another eighteen percent held professional or technical positions and another fifteen percent were craftsmen or mechanics. The most important fact is that the trend in riders is toward an older, more experienced, better educated one, with a better than average household income.

The average Harley riders are all the above, but probably have more of a pro-American attitude. (This is not meant as a slight to any brand, race or country.) They are typically more independent and more involved in the grassroots motorcyclist organizations which watch out for motorcyclists' rights and have a tendency to be more involved in a motorcycling lifestyle. There is most likely a tradition of American bike ownership in their families as well, and they have the strongest brand loyalty at the same time.

The difference in the Harley riders is often seen in their attitude about helmet laws as well. They are much more likely to be anti-helmet or pro-choice than the average rider. There are many subtle reasons for this which are difficult to explain to the non-rider. Simply stated, the Harley riders are more apt to ride for the sheer pleasure of riding and not necessarily worry about their destination. They are more likely to ride "in" their environment (feel it—rather than pass through it) and usually do so at a more leisurely pace than the average sport bike rider. The analogy might be likened to a quarter horse in the woods compared to a race horse at the track; or an open pick-up truck in the country compared to an exotic convertible sports car in the city.

Not every Harley rider fits this description and certainly other riders of other brands may fit the mold, but the tendency to enjoy "the wind in your hair" is stronger. Non-riders can probably relate to other outdoor sports which have similar feelings of freedom and wind in the hair—bicycle riding, sailing, horseback riding and skiing are just a few.

TWO SIDES TO EVERY STORY

The topics discussed by the proponents of mandatory helmet legislation are very similar to the topics brought up by those against mandatory helmet legislation. They both, however, feel very differently about the topics. In the paragraphs that follow, I will try to share the thoughts of both sides of the debate. The following items are topics often discussed:

The proponent viewpoint:

1) "Helmets are just like seat belts. If you wear a helmet you are less likely to have injuries and fatalities—just like seat belts in a car."

2) "It doesn't look safe to ride a motorcycle without a helmet."

3) "There are fewer injuries and fatalities for helmeted riders."

4) "Motorcyclists are a public burden. Victims of motorcycle accidents are more likely to have head injuries than automobile drivers, and their injuries cost more than the average automobile driver's. Accidents don't just affect the rider—we have to pay for their hospital and rehabilitation care."

5) "Helmets don't affect your hearing, comfort (temperature), or visual senses (like peripheral vision) and anyway, most accidents happen from a frontal angle (between eleven and one o'clock)."

6) "It's obvious that helmeted riders are safer and therefore must take less risks."

Freedom of choice advocates:

The usual answer for the previous six statements would probably go as follows:

1) "Helmets aren't like seat belts. Seat belts are part of the automobile and aren't an item of wearing apparel. Seat belts don't have to be carried around with you when you get to your destination like a bowling ball. If seat belts are

the solution to preventing injuries and fatalities, why are head injuries the most common injury and cause of death in automobile accidents? Why are fatality and injury rates on the rise for automobile drivers when there are mandatory seat belt laws in most of the nation?"

2) "It doesn't feel safe to wear a helmet. I feel isolated from my surroundings."

3) "The data is inconclusive in most studies that deal with motorcyclist injuries and fatalities. It isn't usually known or stated how many in the study were even wearing a helmet at the time of their accident. The important statistics deal with the number of injuries or fatalities per 100 accidents. States with no helmet laws have twenty percent fewer accidents. If helmets are the cure-all they are supposed to be, why don't states with mandatory helmet laws for everyone have substantially fewer accidents per 10,000 registration and fewer injuries and fatalities per 100 accidents?"

4) "Head injuries are the most common injury for pedestrians (more of whom die each year than motorcyclists), bicyclists, automobile drivers and their passengers. A head injury is a head injury and the costs are the same for that injury regardless of the way you received it. The public pays or is burdened by all types of welfare or medical care, regardless of the cause or type of trauma. The list is endless—smoking, obesity, heart disease, old age, etc. The public certainly wouldn't be asked to wear helmets in cars or as pedestrians because of public burden. Why should motorcyclists be singled out?"

5) "Motorcyclists opposed to mandatory helmet laws say that helmets can contribute to the cause of accidents. It should be self-evident that covering your ears, restricting your peripheral vision and limiting the range of motion of your head would impair your perceptions. Why are helmets illegal to use in cars in most states and why do manufacturers' stickers in some helmets say that helmets are not designed to prevent head injuries beyond thirteen miles per hour. Borrow a friend's helmet on a hot day and try wearing one for several hours. Ride a bicycle, drive your car or just walk around your house or office. Then you can fairly make your own decision about whether there is any sensory impairment."

6) "There is no conclusive proof regarding the risk factors of helmeted versus non-helmeted riders, as most medical studies fail to separate helmeted riders from non-helmeted riders in their studies. Riders who wear helmets have a false sense of security and take more chances than the non-helmeted rider."

THE HISTORY OF THE CONTROVERSY

From the dawn of the American motorcycle experience, in the early 1900s, every conceivable piece of wearing apparel was used by the early pioneer motorcycle riders to keep the bad weather elements out while riding. For the most part, American roadways, in this era, were little more than dirt or oiled rural fire roads, and riders were constantly subjected to personal discomfort, and at worst, run off roads by superior-minded automobile drivers. The American motorcycles of these early years, Aces, Hendersons, Indians, and Harley-Davidsons (among others) were relatively slow and lumbering. This was just as well, considering the average road conditions their riders encountered. There was little thought given to donning anything resembling a helmet for head protection in a fall. Plastic was yet to be widely used, except for the material from which telephones were made. For protection from rain, snow, sleet, cold and the elements, leather aviator caps and woolen watch caps were popular, as they continue to be today.

After World War II, the government began to invest its "peace dividend" into improving the country's roadway infrastructure. It grew up around the burgeoning suburbs which were needed to house millions of returning veterans and their families, and to deal with America's exploding population boom. As road conditions improved, motorcycle sales began to rise significantly. Motorcycling evolved from a relatively cheap means of transportation to an enjoyable way of getting from point A to point B. In the late 1950s, plastic motorcycle helmets made their appearance and occasional use of them began to be seen.

Two significant events shaped the inevitable attempts, by the federal government to force universal mandatory motorcycle helmet use for all riders, and the predictable bitter struggle by freedom-loving individualists to oppose them. In the late 1950s and early 1960s, British motorcycle manufacturers began making unprecedented inroads into the American motorcycle market. Names such as Matchless, Triumph, Velocette, BSA, Norton, Ariel, Vincent, Royal Enfield, and AJS began to appear on the gas tanks of light, quick, sporting motorcycles, designed by their English manufacturers to appeal to American riders, challenging Harley-Davidson, the sole American motorcycle survivor. The British motorcycles were very sporty and fast, by those contemporary standards, and at least as reliable as their American counterparts. Motorcycle sales skyrocketed.

By the late 1950s the second motorcycle phenomenon reached American shores. Small, almost toylike motor scooters and small displacement motorcycles from Japan began to appear in dealers' showrooms, almost as an accessory item. However, more and more people began buying these oddities, and started to share the motorcycling experience. With so many new riders, the inevitable increase in motorcycle accidents began to be noticed by bureaucrats in state and federal governments. Few states even required a separate license for motorcycle riders until the mid-1960s, creating the perfect environment for motorcycle carnage. Motorcyclist-involved accident rates shot up, with riders having no formal training or education about their machines' behavior, no minimal licensing procedures, and riding modern motorcycles whose power had exceeded their braking, handling, and operating capabilities.

All over the United States, safety officials and state legislators watched with concern as fatality totals from motorcycle accidents continued to increase during the early 1960s. A Washington state accident summary published in 1967 showed that two-thirds of all Washington motorcycle fatalities in 1965 and 1966 resulted from head injury. In 1966, New York, Michigan, and Georgia adopted helmet use laws. Later that year, the U.S. Department of Health, Education and Welfare published preliminary data suggesting that motorcycle fatalities would be reduced by forty percent if all motorcyclists used helmets. After evaluation of this and other evidence, the National Highway Traffic and Safety Administration (NHTSA) included a motorcycle safety standard as one of the initial thirteen Highway Safety Program Standards issued in June of 1967. Under this standard, states were required to provide that each motorcycle operator and passenger wear an approved safety helmet. Then President Lyndon Johnson had also proposed a universal helmet law as part of his omnibus Highway Safety Act in 1965.

The Highway Safety Act of 1966 authorized the federal government to set minimum standards for state highway safety programs. The same act also authorized the government to withhold ten percent of federal highway construction funds and all federal highway safety funds from any state which failed to comply with these standards. In 1967, the secretary of commerce issued thirteen highway safety standards, one of which was for motorcycle safety. One part of the motorcycle standard required the states to enact mandatory motorcycle helmet use laws.

Although motorcycles had been in use in this country for more than eighty years, their popularity had grown dramatically since the early 1960s. With the growth in motorcycle use had come evidence that head injuries were the leading cause of death in motorcycle accidents, according to NHTSA. NHTSA also alleged that according to their evidence, motorcycle safety helmets were an effective means of reducing the incidence and severity of head injuries in motorcycle accidents.

In 1966, Georgia became the first state to require helmet use by law. By the time the motorcycle safety standard was issued, eleven states had already passed helmet use laws. By the close of 1969, forty states had adopted legislation requiring helmet use. The number of states adopting helmet legislation continued to grow, and by 1975, helmet use was required of all motorcyclists in forty-seven states, the District of Columbia and Puerto Rico. That year, the secretary of transportation began proceedings against California, Illinois, and Utah, to determine whether the highway safety programs of those states should be disapproved because of the states' failure to require helmet use by all motorcyclists, even though Secretary Coleman was quoted as saying, "I think that provi-

sion (mandatory helmet use) doesn't make sense, but I have to follow the law." Disapproval of the states' highway safety programs could have led to the withholding of federal funds ($50 million, in California's case). Rumor had it that California's governor then, Ronald Reagan, threatened to shut down every federal agency office in California, if appropriated highway fund money was actually withheld from his state.

Before the secretary could act, however, Congress passed the Highway Safety Act of 1976. Senators Cranston's and Helms' amendment to Section 208(a) of that act removed the secretary's authority to require the states to adopt helmet laws, thereby preventing the secretary from imposing financial sanctions on any state that repealed its law. To underline the point, this section also removed the secretary's authority to withhold ten percent of a state's highway construction funds for failing to implement any of the standards declared under the act.

State legislatures were pressed shortly after to take advantage of the Congressional action. By 1979, twenty-seven states had either fully repealed their helmet laws, or revised them so that only motorcyclists under eighteen were required to wear helmets. According to NHTSA, "During this period, the number of deaths from motorcycle accidents jumped significantly from 3,312 in 1976 to 4,850 in 1979. The 1979 figure represents an increase of forty-six percent over 1976." NHTSA conveniently omitted mentioning that one of the largest three-year increases in motorcycle registrations occurred in that same period from 1976 to 1979, with an increase of almost 750,000 new motorcycles (representing a fifteen percent increase) being registered. Total motor vehicle registrations increased also, in those three years, by seventeen million.

The decade of the 1980s began to reflect the reality of motorcycle safety in the United States. Mandatory helmet laws were not the panacea their proponents claimed. Education, training and motorist awareness programs, not helmet laws, began making a significant statistical difference in reducing motorcycle accidents nationwide.

By the end of 1989, twenty-three states had helmet laws for all motorcycle riders, and twenty-four states had modified helmet laws covering some segment of those states' riders (but not adults). Four states had no helmet laws for anyone. States with full helmet laws regularly did not have *significantly* lower fatality rates per accident (the only true statistical barometer of helmet use effectivity) than states with modified helmet laws. Indeed, states with no helmet laws for anyone had five to ten percent lower fatality rates than helmet law states.

As the end of the 1980s approached, thirty-two states had enacted some form of motorcycle training and education, prior to licensing. Much to the disappointment of those who feel that only mandatory helmet laws will reduce motorcycle fatalities, death rates dropped a phenomenal thirty percent nationally during the 1980s, despite over half of the nation's motorcycle riders living in states with no helmet laws for adult riders. These welcome reductions in motorcycle accidents are even more amazing as the total number of motor vehicles in the United States rose by 23 million, or twelve percent, during this same period. It is estimated that automobile drivers cause over fifty percent of all motorcycle accidents. In spite of the fact that motorcycle riders were competing with 23 million more automobiles than in the last decade, motorcycle deaths are down by thirty percent.

There is some disagreement as to the reasons for this dramatic accident decline, but one factor is certainly not responsible for it—mandatory helmet laws for all riders. As we begin the 1990s, those favoring arguably effective helmet laws are on the offensive. Two bills supporting national mandatory motorcycle helmet usage are being considered, and many states are preparing to introduce similar anti-motorcyclist legislation. Those who believe in one's "freedom of choice" will continue to oppose any such discriminatory legislation. As Benjamin Franklin so aptly stated over 200 years ago, "They, that can give up essential liberty to obtain a little safety, deserve neither liberty nor safety."

WHY DOES THIS ISSUE GENERATE SUCH STRONG FEELINGS AMONG MOTORCYCLISTS?

Independent of our personal stance or position on the issue, there must be an explanation for why thirty states have modified or rescinded their mandatory helmet laws. The laws of inertia apply to legislation with the same undeniable result as those laws have on physical objects. In the absence of a significant force, all of those mandatory helmet laws adopted in the mid-1960s would still be on the books.

Where did that force come from? Why did people opposed to mandatory helmet use feel so strongly about this issue? There are many answers to that question but they can generally be grouped under two major headings: (1) freedom of choice and (2) the drawbacks of helmet use.

The first of these reasons is easy to understand. Most people would rather make their own decisions than have their options replaced by governmental direction. Many of those most active in the efforts to maintain or regain freedom of choice are veterans, many of whom served at posts around the world to protect rights of "self-determination." The idea of having important decisions made for you and imposed on you, often by people with no real knowledge of or experience with the subject at hand, runs counter to the basic assumption that this is a free country.

But why the second reason? Are there really drawbacks to helmet use, and what are they? For those who have never ridden a motorcycle, and especially for those who have never worn a motorcycle helmet, there is a tendency to discount arguments that there are real disadvantages to wearing a helmet. If helmets are the panacea to the problem why are so many of those most directly affected by mandatory helmet laws so strongly opposed to them?

Maybe there are drawback to helmets. Maybe a law requiring helmets for all riders in all situations is not the answer to improving motorcycle safety. The states with mandatory helmet laws have more accidents per 10,000 registrations than the states with partial or no helmet laws. And even more noteworthy, the states with no helmet laws or partial helmet laws (non-adult) have lower injury and fatality rates. Maybe there are alternative solutions which will provide better results.

AN ALTERNATIVE SOLUTION

If mandatory helmet laws aren't the answer to improved motorcycle safety, what is? The recent experience of California and other states with mandatory training programs is illuminating to say the least. The plain fact is, if you fall off a motorcycle you will probably get hurt. A helmet cannot prevent an accident. Whether a helmet can mitigate injury, and to what degree, are subjects of substantial disagreement. However, the object should be not to fall off or have an accident in the first place.

Using California's recent experience is a good example. In 1986 California enacted legislation for mandatory rider education. Called the California Motorcyclist Safety Program, it required all applicants under eighteen years of age to complete a rider training course in order to receive a motorcycle license. According to the California Highway Patrol, this program is one of the key factors in achieving the remarkable reduction in injuries and fatalities in California over the last three years.

Since 1986, motorcycle injuries and fatalities have decreased in California by thirty-four percent and twenty-eight percent respectively. During this period the number of registered motorcycles has decreased somewhat, but has been more than offset by the increase in licensed riders. During the same period (with a new seat belt law in effect), automobile injuries and fatalities have each increased by fifteen percent.

The experience throughout the nation has been similar where rider education and training programs exist. Thousands and thousands of riders have benefited from the program and passed on the lessons learned to their friends. Interestingly enough there is one thing that the pro-helmet camp and pro-choice camp do agree on—and that's the importance of rider education. Maybe legislators everywhere should listen to those who ride . . . and let them decide!

THE QUESTION OF BROTHERHOOD

By Keith R. Ball

Bikers are not unique to this age, nor is their bond of brotherhood. Since men have struggled against the elements, there have been a restless few who would not accept conventional social limits, warriors who fought on all frontiers for all forms of freedom, renegades who could not accept the norms of comfortable existence. Such men have always stood apart, as do bikers today.

All bikers don't ride motorcycles. The man who builds a 30-foot, full-keel ketch and sails around the world belongs to the biker brotherhood, for he is one more individualist, one more man walking head-on into a wall of obstacles and not taking no for an answer until he has achieved his purpose. A man who makes a statement with his life, rather than simply surviving it.

Warriors, seamen, pilots, and race car drivers belong to this kingdom, a round table of men who want more out of life even if they must take it by force, must break rules to claim their lives as their own, or must risk their lives to feel they have earned them.

Bikers may not get along with every fist-fightin', stubborn, loud-mouthed, nonconformist of their own kind that they meet, but they understand him, for they share a common bond that itself perpetuates the brawls, the arguments, and competitions that arise whenever they meet.

Bikers may seem earthy, peasants of the wheel rather than the plow, but the kingdom harbors its fair share of men in suits and white shirts, whether the one motorcycle dealer who mustered 10,000 riders for a bone-chilling, November Muscular Dystrophy ride; or Malcolm Forbes, who built a multimillion dollar publishing industry by ignoring the conventional wisdom; or the handful of men who stuck together to pull Harley-Davidson through a decade of crises to keep America's only motorcycle manufacturer alive. They're bikers.

A man may see his destiny in many ways, but if he has the bravery to follow it he will find it a lonely existence, for the corollary of individuality is aloneness. Like the sailor navigating the Pacific single-handedly, a biker will often find himself alone on an empty highway, wondering why the hell he is out there, spitting sand out of his teeth, entirely alone. Like the sailor, the biker spends those hours alone because an adventure lies at the end of the road, and the trip is discovery of the greatest enigma—himself.

In a poem I read recently, a kid asked his dad if everything he bought for his motorcycle made him a biker. The father tried to explain that being a biker had nothing to do with possessions. Bikers are born, not taught. Warriors are born, not trained. The spirit is something in the eyes, a desire that runs from the opening of the pupils to the depths of the soul.

It's the same spirit that makes a man build an airplane in the back yard and test it against the elements, the spirit that provokes a man to spend a year getting his hands full of splinters building a boat to sail across the Pacific.

The same desire grabbed a sixteen year old I knew. His parents, strict as a company of drill sergeants and narrow as a picket fence, despised motorcyclists. His first vehicle was a motorcycle which he didn't hide from them. Rather, he bought it with his own earnings and brought it proudly home.

But that first bike wasn't enough. Between tours of duty in Vietnam, he had to have a Harley-Davidson, and a brand new, factory-fresh bike would not do. To feel his own unique spirit as a man, the bike had to be distinctly his own. The desire to build began with the mild customization of that ride, and grew with the purchase of a ex-cop bike and working with an old builder to find the key to the internal workings of the engine. He learned and ultimately built his own engine. He taught himself how to dismantle and assemble complete motorcycles. He studied the electronics, the driveline, and oil systems. He researched the written word on finishes, then found a mentor to show him how the written words could be translated into the preparation, molding, and painting of his own bike and those of his brothers.

But craftsmanship was not the sole purpose of the exercise. The purpose was to ride, and he rode—to work, for entertainment, and also for peace of mind. His hair grew, and so did his beard. Wherever he went, he remained a proud biker, proud of the way he looked, proud the way a mountain man took pride in the hair down his back, proud the way a commando felt about the beard that grew during a month's underground duty, proud of his motorcycle, which he built and would live and die with, and proud of his aggressive ability, that demanded the most of himself and the bike he put together with his own hands. He was a man who lived to ride and rode to live.

He never asked whether he was a biker or not.

As a lover, he chose women who dreamt of fast nights and sunlit highways to caress their desires. As an artist, he took a welding torch as his instrument. As a fighter, he chose a chromed wide glide with highbars as his weapons against lanes of jagged fools. And as a profession, he found a way to help men who shared his feelings about motorcycles and themselves and he worked to keep the lifestyle alive.

It's not something a man or a woman asks about, studies to become, or hopes to graduate to. It's in the heart and the soul—Ride on.

A NON-RIDER'S PERSPECTIVE

By Susan Carmona

When my husband conceived the idea for this book he had a particular reader in mind; the non-riding public. It was his feeling, and I had to agree, that non-riders have some rather negative perceptions of motorcyclists, primarily Harley-Davidson bikers. Because I am not a biker, but married to one, has provided me an opportunity not many non-riders have to see and experience both sides of the bike, so to speak.

I understand how the non-riding public could hold biased views and perceptions of biking. I don't mean to imply that all non-riders regard bikers in a less than positive light, but I've spoken with enough of you to know that many mirror what *were* my exact feelings. It's because of those findings that I was able to convince my spouse to allow me this space in the book to share some of those feelings in hopes that someone may relate and gain insight by reading about where I've been and where I've come in my quest for biker understanding.

When I say I experienced caution and apprehension toward bikers it's not an exaggeration. I always wondered about what made them tick but never quite knew how to go about finding out. To actually go to the source and ask was never a consideration. Bikers seemed to own a certain mystique and badness that was the source of my intimidation and intrigue. This did not apply to all motorcyclists because all motorcyclists did not qualify as "bikers." This applied to the small sect of riders that would resemble my idea of what motorized intruders from the underworld, perhaps Hades, might look like. You know the ones I mean: they're mean looking and garbed in black leather, tattoos and headbands, often carrying women passengers you know must be as bad and vicious as they are on their obtrusive machines. The type that devalue your real estate holdings by their mere presence.

I remember the difference in comfort I experienced when a kid wearing shorts and a tank top, riding a generic-looking motorcycle pulled up next to my car versus the time I observed (through my rearview mirror) a pack of bikers clad in leather nearing to invade my space. Big difference. The kid in the shorts represented no threat, but evoked more of a parental concern for his skin and its protection. With the bikers my only concern was to stay out of their way. I found myself visually guarded so not to make actual eye contact, but rather time it just right so as they passed I could make a private observation. Do my reactions sound strange? Well, stranger yet is I had no bad personal experiences or encounters with bikers. I just knew I didn't like them. It wasn't until recently that I began to ask myself why.

We've had some help from the outside in fortifying our negative thinking. For instance, when was the last time you watched a movie that depicted bikers as upright and moral citizens? Most likely they were portrayed as hell-raising, rabble-rousing, social outcasts. We didn't get where we are by ourselves. We've had some impressive help. What I have discovered is that I've perceived these bikers wrongly and judged them too harshly. Yes, some of them look pretty wild and inapproachable and a few might very well be, but had I not married a respected business man who transforms into one of these biker characters I just described, and found myself as the woman passenger, I'm afraid I never would have realized and discovered that "normal" people like you and me make up the majority of riders. I don't want to ruffle anyone's feathers here, so I'm going to add that there are those out there and in this book that were born bikers. They live and breathe bikes and have loved Harley and the biker world from the get-go. I have a lot of respect for you because you're the ones that have kept this sport going and surviving for "nouveau bikers" and hopefuls like myself. Thanks.

As a non-rider you might be asking yourself why the Harley rider, if he's such a good guy, seemingly dresses to promote the "bad boy" image. Valid question. There's no simple answer. The leather worn is primarily done so for protection. If a rider goes down on his bike, leather clothing is really the only raiment that will hold up and protect him. The style bikers choose to wear is also designed with the elements in mind. Boots are the best protection for feet because they cover the ankle and upper leg. Some bikers wear chaps for added protection, but mostly, they are worn to ward off the cold. It's a lot different on a bike than in the enclosed compartment of an automobile. As for tattoos and headbands, etc., who knows? Different strokes for different folks. Some bikers want to look bad; that's part of being a biker, too. As long as you remember that bikers are not out to "get" you and are good guys, what's the harm or need to know all the why's? They ride in packs because they're safer on the roads that way; car operators can see them more easily, plus they enjoy riding with pals. Why are Harleys so loud? That's just part of what makes Harley-Davidson motorcycles so unique. It's a characteristic of the machine and belongs only to Harley. Bikers love the sound of their Harleys and would gladly make them louder if it were legally permissible. I hope this has been helpful in shedding some light on a few of your why's.

Perhaps you've considered riding a motorcycle but don't have one, or maybe are married to a person that does but won't let you near it even after you've pleaded and promised not to drop or scratch it, in which case, I strongly suggest you do what I did: enroll in your local Motorcycle Safety Course! I can't recommend this course enough to non-riders. You'll receive professional supervision from highly trained and capable instructors who will take a person with absolutely no hands-on experience and get you up and riding by gradual step-by-step practical instruction. They provide the bike and, I might add, will not yell at you if you drop or scratch it!

One of the added benefits to taking this course is the discount you will receive on your motorcycle insurance when you provide your carrier with your course completion certificate. If you don't know if you have a course in your area, contact the Department of Motor Vehicles and they'll be able to furnish you with information. Many bikers have taken both the beginning and advanced safety courses just to keep sharp and get as much training under their belts as possible. To receive training in a controlled environment versus getting your own experience on the streets are two very different ways of education. Most riders prefer the training.

Harley-Davidson gave us a wonderful gift besides a magnificent piece of machinery. They gave bikers a world that affords people from all walks of life a common ground. I have witnessed the biker double-back and go out of his way to help a fellow Harley rider who had encountered some problem on the road; both total strangers to each other. I have met the mechanic and the millionaire, lightyears apart in their day-to-day existence, share a bond in riding without discrimination (from either side) as to net worth, race, or gender. They both share the same love and pride for their bikes and the sport of motorcycling. In my opinion, it's all of this that gives special significance to the "brotherhood" of Harley-Davidson.

I hope the next time a biker pulls up alongside your car you'll remember this book and the interviews and stories in it. Bikers are doing and enjoying what they love: riding to feel free and enjoying their freedom to ride. Who knows, that biker next to you might very well be me, and although I'm a sweetheart I'll be wearing my leathers and lookin' bad. It just goes to show you . . . you just never know!

WOMEN AND MOTORCYCLES—What a Concept!

By Sarah Faraday

Women and motorcycles—what a concept! The mere thought of women and motorcycles only five years ago would have made the hair stand up on any two-legged beast but times have changed, so have women, so have motorcycles.

Although there's a tremendous surge of women in motorcycling today, this is not a new concept. Women have been riding motorcycles for nearly a century when the first bikes hit the cobblestones in the late 1800s. It may not have been as popular then as it is now, but as in all concepts, it had to start somewhere.

Women who ride today owe their gratitude to such pioneers as Clara Wagner who in 1907 became the first woman member in the Federation of American Motorcyclists (FAM—similar to the AMA today) and the first woman in America to win a competitive motorcycle event, although denied the trophy because she was a woman. Effie Hotchkiss and her mother, Avis, became the first women to cross the United States, on a Harley-Davidson V-Twin and sidecar rig in 1915 and in 1916. Augusta and Adeline Van Buren became the first women to cross the continent on two Indian Power Plus solo motorcycles. It took them *only* three months.

Although women have been riding for years, it's only recently that it has become a phenomenon. The question remains, why now?

In a society where women have had to try twice as hard to accomplish anything and even harder to be accepted, motorcycling became another domain demanding challenge and acceptance. Moving from the back of the bike to the front was the first step.

As women began leaving the kitchen to build careers of their own while still raising families, they discovered a whole new world of adventure. Riding motorcycles, among other things, became a natural progression in exercising their new-found independence. Not only did they discover the excitement and fun of today's motorcycling, but also learned that riding in the wind after a long, stressful week induced total mental relaxation.

Women have become the fastest-growing segment of the motorcycle market today, a phenomenon and trend expected to continue. In a time when motorcycle sales are declining, women just may be the saving grace for the industry.

More than half a million women are riding their own machines today, and it is estimated that by 1993, twenty percent of the riding population will be women.

Oddly enough, motorcycling has always been thought of as a young person's sport. No longer true. The average age for a woman to start riding her own bike today is thirty-five years old. By the time she is thirty-eight, most women are riding 1000cc bikes or larger. The reasons are simple. Most women in their twenties are getting married, having children, just starting their careers or don't make enough disposable income yet to purchase a bike and the necessary accessories. It seems by the time a woman is in her thirties, she has accomplished many of these things and is ready for new and exciting adventures, one being the personal challenge of motorcycling.

Motorcycle Safety Foundation instructors around the country report that forty-two to fifty percent of their classrooms are now filled with women. They also claim that women make better students because they're more receptive to learning. Women have proven to be more safety conscious and even balance motorcycles better than men simply because of their physical difference in center of gravity placement.

To be a woman in motorcycling today is to some degreee to still be a pioneer. For this reason few companies make motorcycle clothing for women, making it difficult to find attractive and comfortable riding gear. But, that's finally changing. Both manufacturing and accessory companies have taken notice of the growth and are finally designing products more conducive to women's needs.

It is because of this growth that publisher Courtney Caldwell created a publication specifically geared toward women, *American Woman Road Riding* magazine. It was designed to fill the need for communication among the growing number of women riders and to dispel the myth that women who ride motorcycles were less than ladylike.

Women riders want information. They want to learn the how to's and how not to's. They want to know where and how to get products without being taken to the cleaners. And, they want to hear it from another woman, one that can relate to their experiences in a language they can understand. This is one reason why Caldwell's seminars, entitled *Women and Motorcycles—A New Direction* are always packed at the national rallies.

Today's woman rider is sharp and sophisticated. She is a career woman, a mother, a grandmother, a business owner, a homeowner, an adventuress. She's exactly the kind of girl you'd take home to mother. Women in motorcycles—what a concept!

THE FUTURE

A friend of mine once said to me when we were riding, "Carmen, this feels so good,
I wonder why they haven't made it illegal."
Let's all work together to make sure they never do.

INDEX

ORDERING INFORMATION

To order additional copies of *The Iron Stallion* contact:

Hirshberg Publishing, Inc.
11110 Ohio Ave., Suite 104
Los Angeles, CA 90025
(213) 473-7223
FAX: (213) 312-1773